NORTHERN DELIGHTS

SCANDINAVIAN HOMES, INTERIORS AND DESIGN

gestalten

HOTEL MAGAZINET
Gotland, Sweden
INTERIOR STYLIST: Sofie Ganeva, CLIENT: Fantastic Frank,
PHOTOGRAPHER: Kristofer Johnson

Classic twentieth-century design by the great masters like Jacobsen and Aalto can be seen all over Scandinavia, in public places, schools, airports, kindergartens, and restaurants. We grow up surrounded by it, and in this way it becomes a part of our subconscious preferences. The simple shapes of bentwood furniture, high-quality craftsmanship and light colors are so deeply rooted in the back of our minds that it becomes almost unthinkable to furnish our homes in a different way. This is probably why it is common practice in Denmark that when you buy your first apartment you extend the loans a bit to be able to also get some design classics to furnish your new home with.

NORTHERN DELIGHTS is all about the calm, reduced, nature-related, and well-crafted lifestyle. The first words that come to mind are often light, simple, and natural but there is more behind this style than that. The first rule of Scandinavian design is that form follows function; everything should be practical above all. But there is no need to compromise on style because of this, as the idea that even mass-produced everyday items should have an aesthetic value has been adopted here since the end of the nineteenth century. At this time factories around Scandinavia started hiring artists to enhance the beauty of their products as a step towards the goal of raising the population's living standards, by providing good products and homes for all.

The classic design icons, like for example the Ant and Seven chairs, Tulip tables, AJ lamps and Aalto's birch stools, all share some common factors; they have clean lines, high quality, great ergonomics, and a timelessness that never goes out of style.

THESE PRODUCTS WILL LAST YOU A LIFETIME BECAUSE OF THEIR ABILITY TO EASILY BE MATCHED WITH NEWER DESIGNS.

and they will never look out of place no matter what you surround them with. The high quality of the materials and craftsmanship will also guar-

antee that they will age with grace, making them good investments. These are probably some of the factors that have made Scandinavian design so popular, especially in the last few years with the recession forcing people to carefully evaluate and consider what they buy. What made them popular in the first place though, back in the 1940s and 1950s when they were first made, was the fact that they were truly revolutionary. Not only stylewise, as a big step away from the more ornate furniture of the past decades, but also technically.

These were the first truly mass-produced furniture pieces, and techniques such as bending wood and molding plastic had never been used in these ways before. Mass production also meant lower prices, so the designs were available to a big part of the population, not only the well-off upper classes. The quality of the designs was still kept very high though, with a big part of the construction still being made by hand. This new way of manufacturing furniture also played a big part in the style of the designs, enabling simpler lines and lighter framework, which has since come to signify the Scandinavian style.

Today's designers have a great heritage to base their work on, and the lines and styles from the older design can be seen clearer in some designs than others. Many brands, like Artek, Fritz Hansen, Hay, and Gubi, that have been around since the beginning of the last century are also re-releasing old designs that were previously taken off the market or have never been produced until now. However, there is also a new and contemporary Scandinavian style, with a focus on new materials and an even more simplistic view of design. In this group you will find young talents such as Nina Bruun, Daniel Rybakken, and Clara von Zweigbergk. Their experimental work sometimes borders on art, and coming directly out of design schools they have the freedom to occasionally let usability give way to more poetic values.

A strong commitment to high quality runs through the entire society up here in the north. Everything from fashion to food is viewed through the same lens, where making something functional into something beautiful is always the main goal. At a smaller scale, Scandinavian living in private homes is also signified by durability, affordability, practicality, and sustainability. Gardens are places for growing vegetables, as well

as spaces to play and enjoy beautiful flowers. For those living in apartments, with no access to a garden, allotment gardens are common in the bigger cities to provide everyone with the possibility of growing their own crops. Kitchens are bright and planned according to well-proved rules, and used for crafting, homework, and socializing as well as cooking. Floors are made from pine or oak, often painted in light hues or oiled to provide a durable and warm surface which also reflects the much coveted light.
The most prominent feature of the Scandi style is the love of light and simplicity.

LIGHT IS PROBABLY THE SINGLE MOST IMPORTANT FACTOR IN THE NORDIC HOME.

As we have such short summers, and long dark winters, letting in and reflecting as much light as possible into our homes becomes a priority. This is where the white walls come from, along with the big windows and light-colored furniture.
The massive amount of candles used in Scandinavia all year round certainly also has something to do with trying to chase away the darkness as best we can.
Scandinavian houses always include natural materials like wood and stone, but the proportions of the respective materials vary due to local

BUNAD BLANKET
Oslo, Norway
DESIGNER: Andreas Engesvik

STUGA, SWEDEN

Little red painted wooden houses—called *Stuga*—determine the Swedish countryside und still inspire designers and architects today. They are basing their work on the old traditions of the rural farming society, with simple homemade wooden furniture. Pinewood floors and soft colors in the style of artists Carl and Karin Larsson, the "inventors" of Swedish style, are still popular almost 100 years after their passing.

HYGGE, DENMARK

Danes have a strong focus on giving their spaces a relaxed, cozy, and welcoming look, and they even have their own word summarizing all this: *hygge*. This style includes lots of textiles in the form of cushions, blankets, and rugs, but still with a firm foot in Scandinavian simplicity. Candles are also an essential part of *hygge*, and so are fireplaces, sheepskins, and nice rustic food enjoyed in the relaxed company of friends and family.

Despite all those subtleties, there is also something that can be described as an overall, even international, Nordic style. Similar aesthetics can be found in South Africa, Berlin, or Manhattan. This is partly an effect of our globalized way of living, where everything is available to buy on travels or over the internet, but also a sign of the massive impact that Scandinavian design has made on the world through its talented representatives in design and architecture. The simplicity and muted tones seems to have a universal attraction, and can blend in to any surroundings. Having said this, Nordic interiors show a whole range of different directions, from boho-chic and natural to minimalist concrete industrial and everything in between.

Classic Scandi style, where you find that perfect mix of midcentury Scandinavian design and inherited older pieces, accentuated by a modern detail here and there to add some tension, is the most common way of decorating your home. The older designs, ranging from Gustavian-era side tables and chairs to midcentury teak furniture, work equally well in a turn-of-the century city apartment with high stuccoed ceilings as in a modernist cube of a house.

of the respective materials vary due to local resources. The difference in natural resources is also part of what has shaped the Nordic countries respective interior and furniture styles. Because although they may all look very similar to the untrained eye, each country actually has its own very distinct style, maybe best described by some simple but telling words from each of the languages.

BUNAD, NORWAY

Norway's dramatic landscape with deep woods, long narrow fjords, and high snow-covered mountains is very present in the country's design style and you will see many references to trees or mushroom shapes in the designs produced in the last few years. The patterns and colors of the traditional national costume, the *bunad*, is also a big source of inspiration for young designers.

PELKISTETTY, FINLAND

Leaning on the strong tradition of Aalto and Saarinen, the base of Finnish style lies in simple shapes, strong patterns, and primary colors. Finnish design has no room for unnecessary decorative details. Take a look at their saunas, private or communal, where this style is very obvious. With their wooden interiors, accessorized by nothing more than a bucket of water and a bunch of birch twigs, saunas are the epitome of Finnish style. *Pelkistetty* is Finnish for reduced and simplified.

MATERIALS ARE KEPT TO WARM WOODS SUCH AS BIRCH AND OAK. WALLS ARE PAINTED IN LIGHT, MILD COLORS.

and patterns such as the classic prints of Josef Franck and Marimekko are often seen on both fabrics and wallpaper.

SAUNA AT FOUR CORNERED VILLA
Virrat, Finland
ARCHITECT Avanto Architects

In recent years, one of the big trends is to incorporate rustic or industrial pieces in home decor, with an abundance of natural materials such as stone, leather, wood, and terracotta.
The fabrics are made of rough cotton, wool, or linen and the colors used throughout the homes are kept in hues ranging between white and brown, going through cream, beige, and mole with dashes of black and rust.
Details are brought in both from the surrounding nature and from the industrial world. These could be driftwood, shells, branches, beach pebbles, pine cones, and moss or old factory lamps and tables with a strong patina and a history of their own. Strong contrasts are avoided in favor of harmonious tone-in-tone hues and interest is added by using different textures (for example rough vs. smooth, matte vs. shiny, and sheepskins vs. more delicate fabrics) instead of patterns.

At the other end of the spectrum we have the more minimalist direction, where all unnecessary bits and pieces are banished, but that doesn't have to mean that this style is cold and sterile. To add warmth to the clean lines of their sparely furnished Scandinavian minimalist houses, these homeowners use art, lighting, and the occasional plant or textile detail. Natural wood also softens the impression and could be used for flooring, walls, furniture, or interior details. The idea here is that all accessories should have a function, and nothing is there just because it looks nice, as such things are considered clutter. Nostalgic inherited or gifted pieces are best kept behind closed doors, to keep the look streamlined and practical.

Amongst the young, design-minded Scandinavians, with senses wide open to new materials and solutions, a fresh and eccentric style is developing. Bright splashes of color, spectacular art, and new inventive uses of old objects are some of the things that characterize this development. Here we also find references to the pop art primary colors from the late 1960s/1970s, found in both new products and vintage finds from those decades. Surprising and untraditional, they still have an obvious Nordic tone that can be seen in the use of simple, honest materials and practical choices.

Design in the twenty-first century is about much more than making good-looking objects. The days of oblivious consumerism are over, and sustainability has become a key word for everyone involved, from the manufacturer through to the designer and all the way out to the end consumer. Scandinavian design with its values of good craftsmanship, high quality, and natural materials fits perfectly with this more conscious way of living. It makes any place feel like home.

By Emma Fexeus

Stockholm-based Emma Fexeus, born 1979, works as an interior stylist and writer. In 2005 she started what is now Sweden's oldest and most-read design and deco blog, Emmas Designblogg. It has a focus on homes and interiors and features photos made by the world's leading stylists and photographers. Her style is definitely Scandinavian, but the pictures come from all over the world.

CERAMIC POTS FROM FERM LIVING
Copenhagen, Denmark
DESIGNER & PRODUCER Ferm Living

CLASSIC BEAUTY

A mid-century bench, with a cushion in the classic elephant pattern from Svenskt Tenn placed on top, welcomes you when you walk in the door of this house, built at the turn of the nineteenth century. The ceilings are high and beautifully adorned with ornamental stucco work, creating an interesting contrast to the modern pendant lights. The hallway's parquet flooring is mostly covered by a long striped rag rug, which gives a more relaxed tone to the room. As you step into the living room, you will find a wall covered by art in all sizes, and while the frames are all different, the collection is held together by the color scheme, a simple monochrome theme with many black-and-white photographs and graphic prints. Another wall is lined with tall shelves filled with a mix of books and bits and pieces picked up on travels or inherited from older family members. Next to the Danish 1950s sofa stands one of Alvar Aalto's birch stools, used as both a side table and extra seating, complementing the main sofa table that is a more contemporary piece with a white marble top. The adjoining room, reached through a pair of old paneled double doors, is the combined kitchen and dining room, large and airy with space for many activities. You can see that the owners put lots of care and thought into the renovation, trying to keep as many original details as possible while still keeping it practical for modern family life.

This style is where you will find those typical Scandinavian homes, with white walls and a decor full of twentieth-century design classics mixed with both new and older furniture from flea markets or old relatives. This creates a nice lived-in feeling, and the furniture styles work nicely together, so rather than clashing they just add some interest and a little bit of tension between the pieces. Floors are usually oak parquet or pine boards, often painted or treated with lye to reflect as much light as possible. The big windows are rarely covered by window treatments, fabrics are instead added through cushions, rugs, and wall hangings. These are usually colorful and graphic, a style that can be found from brands like Marimekko and Svenskt Tenn. The same patterns are also often used as wallpaper, but most are satisfied with making feature walls, not covering the entire room as that would give a rather overwhelming expression. The modern pieces found in these homes are rarely cutting-edge designs from young designers, but rather future design classics from top names like Asplund and Artek.

BERMUDA TABLE

Stockholm, Sweden
DESIGNER: **Thomas Eriksson**, PRODUCER: **Asplund**
PHOTOGRAPHER: **Louise Billgert**

Like all of their furniture, Asplund's Bermunda Table, designed by
Thomas Eriksson, is a functional yet entirely light-hearted and
original design. Bermuda's triangular legs are carefully placed according to how people naturally sit at a table, allowing many people
to gather around at once — just right for big dinner parties. The
glossy white table, topped with microeffect finish or Color Core
laminate, can be found at Asplund's store/showroom in Stockholm's central district, along with other handpicked furniture,
textiles, and accessories exemplary of today's Nordic style.

clockwise:

₁FUNK

Storage series
Stockholm, Sweden
DESIGNER: **Per Söderberg**, PRODUCER: **Asplund**

₂ZOO

Mini-tables
Stockholm, Sweden
DESIGNER: **Eero Koivisto**, PRODUCER: **Asplund**

₃TATI

Nesting tables
Stockholm, Sweden
DESIGNER: **Mats Broberg & Johan Ridderstråle**, PRODUCER: **Asplund**

PHOTOGRAPHER: **Louise Billgert**

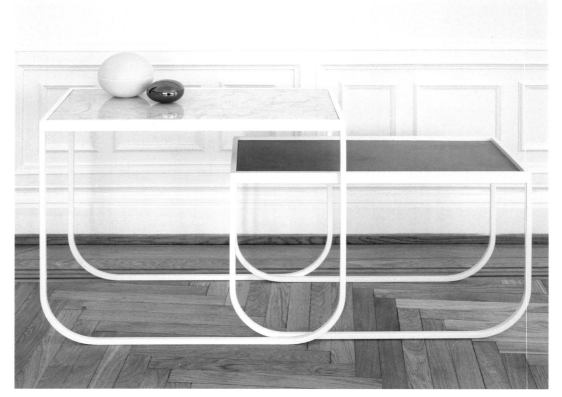

HOERHAVEVEJ
Højbjerg, Aarhus, Denmark
INTERIOR STYLIST: **Mira Wøhlk**, PHOTOGRAPHER: **Tina Stephansen**

Mira Wøhlk's background as an art historian and gallerist lends her a particular eye for design, always seeking optimal composition and finding a balance between content and its expression. Based in Aarhus, Denmark, she is passionate about designing holistic and functional spaces, such as the Hoerhavevej house in her local city. A bastion of Danish functionalism, Hoerhavevej was originally built in 1956, and in 2011 Wøhlk transformed the place into a modern home — combining wood and stone surfaces to retain its Nordic style throughout.

HOERHAVEVEJ

HOME of STEFAN SÖDERBERG

Stockholm, Sweden

PHOTOGRAPHER: **Birgitta Wolfgang Drejer**

It is no wonder that the home of Hope clothing line's creative director, Stefan Söderberg, is as cool, practical, detailed, and comfortable as Hope's garments are. Söderberg's 180-square-meter flat is located in a Stockholm building from 1915, and the space has been redesigned to be more fluid and open. All floors were sandblasted to set the scene for the interior's minimal decor with industrial elements, tastefully decorated with many features from the 1950s, such as timeless Eames furniture, a combination dining work table, and low-hanging copper lamps.

TANJA VIBE

Graphic Designer, ALL THE WAY TO PARIS | Copenhagen, Denmark

REVEALING THE NARRATIVE ELEMENT IN NORDIC DESIGN

Visual storytelling and the poetry of creation are at the heart of All the Way to Paris. A sense of subtlety and playfulness imbues their broad range of projects and clients, ranging from print publications to wallpaper, brand identities, and creative direction. The Copenhagen-based design studio was founded by Danish designer Tanja Vibe and Swedish designer Petra Olsson Gendt in 2004. The two met while working on a magazine project as students at the Royal Danish Academy of Fine Arts School of Design in the 1990s.

They have been collaborating ever since and recently expanded ATWTP to a team of six Danish and Swedish designers. One example of ATWTP's understated aesthetics is the Copenhagen apartment of Tanja Vibe and her husband, Danish artist Ulrick Wick, which served as a setting for the 2012 catalogue of Danish platform Muutu, showcasing the newest talent in new Nordic design.

Why the name "All the Way to Paris"?

For the name of our studio we wanted a name with a narrative approach, one that provokes curiosity in storytelling, which is exactly what graphic design should do. The name "All the Way to Paris" is about storytelling, as well as poetry: the poetry of Paris

is about the exploration of traveling — and most of all, to go "all the way" when designing. It is a reminder to us and our clients to not stop at the first light, but to go all the way.

How would you describe Scandinavian design?

Scandinavian design is usually based on simple, straight-line features: no nonsense, no decoration. Scandinavian design is often based on functionality — hence the simplicity.

How does this reflect in your work and your studio's work?

Our design work is Scandinavian in that it is never decoration without a purpose or

meaning. We work conceptually with all our designs. We do very thorough research and then move on from there. The research may not be noticeable in the design at first glance, but it is there and we hope that it makes the design last a little longer.

You describe your studio as Danish-Swedish. What would you say are some of the differences between the two cultures in terms of design and aesthetics?

Swedish advertising has a strong tradition of clean, Scandinavian graphics. The Danish tradition in architecture and quality design is very strong. The Danes are quick and happy; the Swedes move a bit slower, spending a lot of time thinking before moving. The combination of these two temperaments is very good.

How did being Scandinavian and living in Scandinavia influence the way you furnished your own apartment?

Our Scandinavian aesthetics are reflected in our homes through our love of simplicity, leaving out ornaments and decoration. We both have big families — so function has to be at the center of our sometimes chaotic lives. And yet we're both intrigued by the poetry of life: therefore there is art and well-chosen objects in our simply furnished homes.

What are your favorite (design) pieces at home — and why?

When it comes to our personal surroundings, my favorite items are actually works of art by my husband. His art is often beautiful and reflects his great sense of humor.
One of Petra's favorite pieces at home is her Märta Måås Fjætterström rug. It ties together the room and offers a place where the whole family can relax together in front of the fireplace.
I guess we're both very interested in art rather than design when it comes to living with it.

THIS PAGE:

1 Tanja Vibe and Petra Olsson Gendt, founders of the graphic design studio All the Way to Paris.
2 Graphic identity developed by ATWTP for Stilleben, an interiors and design shop in Copenhagen. The triangle motif can be found on the website, in the shop's interior design, on printed communications, and gift articles.

HOME OF TANJA VIBE

Tanja Vibe's home reflects the design sensibility and
storytelling flair that has helped shape the ATWTP
portfolio. Her home office features vintage Eames
chairs, beat light hanging lamps by Tom Dixon, a bar
cart by Herbert Hirche made by Christian Holzäpfel, an
old painting from the home of her husband's parents,
and a silkscreen print by ATWTP for Circus Hein.

PHOTOGRAPHER: Karina Tengberg

HOME OF TANJA VIBE

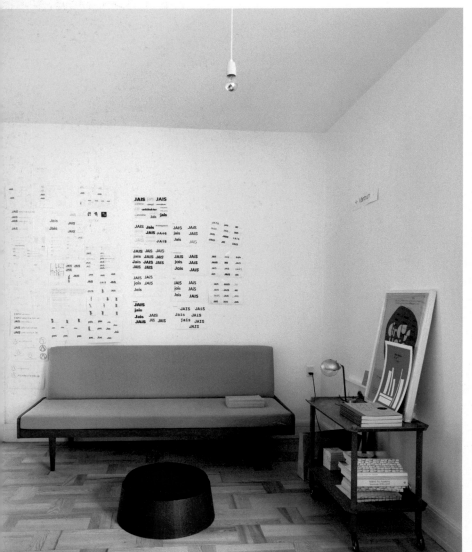

PREVIOUS SPREAD:

Vibe's living room is a comfortable mix of old and new, function and form. With a coffee table from Muuto paired with a Hans J. Wegner sofa, purchased at lauritz.com, a lamp from floss designed by Achille Castiglioni, and an IKEA rug. The neon rainbow is by Vibe's husband, artist Ulrik Weck.

THIS PAGE:

1 Vibe's dining room stands out with its Tom Dixon copper lamps and a stretch of old worktables with chairs by Eiermann and Eames.
2 A place for relaxing creativity: vintage daybed and a small stool by Nana Ditzel. The brass table lamp on the small tea wagon is by Restart Milano.

RIGHT PAGE:

Art and design in dialogue: a photograph by Ulrik is aptly situated above the Louis Poulsen PH lamp that was a gift from his parents.

All images of Tanja Vibe's home by PHOTOGRAPHER: Karina Tengberg

HOME of ULRIKA LUNDGREN

HOME of ULRIKA LUNDGREN

Amsterdam, Netherlands

PHOTOGRAPHER: **Kasia Gatkowska**

"I'm super-Scandinavian in my style," says Ulrika Lundgren, "but I'm influenced by other cultures and the places I go." Just like she does when designing for her fashion label Rika, the Swedish-born, Netherlands-based fashion designer and design maven found a way to blend her urban attitude with a sense of romance when decorating her Amsterdam home. Lundgren stuck to her signature palette of black, white, and cream, splashed with primary colors and toned down by natural woods. The result is a balance of cold, hard lines with warm shapes and light — and several cushioned corners for daydreaming and brainstorming.

VASASTAN APARTMENT

Stockholm, Sweden
INTERIOR STYLIST: **Sofie Ganeva**, CLIENT: **Fantastic Frank**,
PHOTOGRAPHER: **Kristofer Johnssson**

Sofie Ganeva restyled this 64-square-meter apartment situated in the Stockholm city district of Vasastan. Originally built in 1926 in the art nouveau style, the flat has retained elements of its orginal aesthetic with an update according to contemporary Scandinavian sensibility. Preserved details include the large-paned windows with deep niches, a serving aisle, and built-in storage cabinets. A white hardwood floor throughout much of the main space maintains continuity and keeps the space feeling fresh and new.

SOLBRINKEN ORDINARY HOUSE

Stockholm, Sweden
ARCHITECT: **In Praise of Shadows Arkitektur**, DESIGNER: **Katarina Lundeberg**, PHOTOGRAPHER: **Åke E:son Lindman**

The Solbrinken Ordinary House, designed by Katarina Lundeberg with In Praise of Shadows Arkitektur, is a single-family home with a detached studio situated between the forest and a garden in the city of Stockholm. The Swedish architects made the most of the varied landscape and turned a windowless wall towards the neighbors to give the family privacy. In the tradition of Nordic architects like Peter Celsing and Eskil Sundhal, the material palette was kept simple and durable for an active family, using concrete floors, an MDF-clad kitchen, and exterior wood paneling coated with black oil paint — low-key materials in combination with high-quality products.

SOLBRINKEN ORDINARY HOUSE

From 2009 to 2011, Sofia Vusir Jansson ran a store in Katrineholm, Sweden called Mokkasin that sold popular design objects. Now, Jansson has reinvented the store online ("Little Cute Mokkasin"), along with the Mokkasin blog, which has become a sensation for design lovers from around the world. A gifted creator of objects and interiors herself, she frames photographs and prints and artfully arranges them in spaces, builds shelves and drawers, arranges textiles and patterns — and has even built a teepee.

HOME of YVONNE KONÉ

Copenhagen, Denmark
INTERIOR STYLIST: **Stine Langvad**, PHOTOGRAPHER: **Line Klein**

The Copenhagen home of clothing and accessories designer Yvonne Konné was styled by Stine Langvad to embody stark contrasts: light and dark, hard and soft, open space and material density. With deep-hued furniture, lush woods, and minimal accessories, the Danish apartment mirrors the designer's aesthetic impulses for low-key luxury and understated drama.

PLANK
Bergen, Norway
DESIGNER: **Knudsen Berg Hindenes & Myhr MNIL**

The Norwegian designers Knudsen Berg Hindenes designed PLANK sofa inspired by the grandiose Douglas spruce floorboards produced by the Danish flooring company Dinesen. Like Dinesen's lengthy planks, PLANK is made from Douglas spruce, featuring an integrated side table for a form that mirrors Dinesen's long and lean aesthetic. As one of the firm's principal designers, Steinar Hindenes, says: "We aspired to create a floating seat that gives a sense of weightlessness." The weightless effect is certainly achieved.

COLLAGE
Sweden
DESIGNER: **Front**, PRODUCER: **Gemla**

Front created the Collage Chair for Gemla, the oldest furniture manufacturer in Sweden. The chair's wooden frame is bent by hand and its back and seats come in a variety of Swedish leathers, tanned with pine oil, or a choice of textiles.

HOME of NINA BERGSTEN
Malmö, Sweden
PHOTOGRAPHER: **Marcus Lawett**

An avid treasure hunter and design enthusiast who often scavenges flea markets, Nina Bergsten blends her love of vintage pieces with her impeccable taste for modern design items in her own apartment. Touches of gold, mirrors, and pastel colors make this Malmö home a sparing, bright, airy, and feminine abode. Bergsten went to great lengths to create the perfect space — for example, she hired a crane and hoisted a marble tabletop through a window when it would not fit any other way.

HOME of NINA BERGSTEN

HOME of ODDFRID ROPSTAD
Oslo, Norway

PHOTOGRAPHER: **Elisabeth Aarhus**

A young Norwegian designer of costumes and accessories for film and theater, Oddfrid Ropstad found herself the owner of a well-worn and outdated apartment in the Oslo neighborhood of Adamstuen. She set out to fix the place as a Christmas present for both herself and the apartment — single-handedly refurbishing the bright and classic flat with her own flair and eye for design. It now has a gentle atmosphere full of vintage details: a perfect expression of the designer's personal taste and style.

TOWN HOUSE

Landskrona, Sweden

DESIGNER: **Elding Oscarson**, PHOTOGRAPHER: **Åke E:son Lindman**

The narrow site of the townhouse designed by Elding Oscarson is sandwiched between old buildings in Landskrona, Sweden, on a lot that has been empty since around the 1950s. Only five meters wide, the house was designed with a rectilinear approach to maximize the space and to provide a strong contrast with the surrounding buildings on the street. One softly partitioned space spans the width of the house, opened to the street and sky for exposed views and light. With its transparent design and rooftop terrace, the energy-efficient home is a truly modern addition to the community.

HOME of RODE RYBORG
Copenhagen, Denmark
INTERIOR STYLIST: **Julie Vöge**, PHOTOGRAPHER: **Frederikke Heiberg**

The owners of this apartment in the Copenhagen neighborhood
of Frederiksberg, Ditte Rode and her husband Thomas Ryberg
Jørgensen, are both architects. When styling their home, stylist
Julie Vöge incorporated many pieces of the residents' designs, for
example, a clever piece for their children that functions as a bed in
a nook, storage space for toys, and climbing sculpture. Old French
posters combined with nostalgic furniture like a weathered leather
sofa counterbalance the apartment's modern edge.

GRAND PIANO CHAISE LONGUE
and GRÄSHOPPA LAMP
Copenhagen, Denmark
DESIGNER: **Greta M. Grossman / Gubi Olsen**, PRODUCER: **Gubi**

Bo5 – SWING VIP
Denmark
DESIGNER: **Jørgen Gammelgaard**, PRODUCER: **Carl Hansen & Søn**

Carl Hansen & Søn produces classic items by some of Nordic history's best and best-loved designers — from Hans J. Wegner to Mogens Koch to Jørgen Gammelgaard — as well as projects by a new generation of practitioners. The company selects timeless pieces like Gammelgaard's Swing VIP lamp that are still regarded as design icons today. With its classic conic shade and delicate stand, the lamp is instantly recognizable for its history yet melds seamlessly into a modern space.

BESTLITE BL5
Copenhagen, Denmark
DESIGNER: **Robert Dudley Best**, PRODUCER: **Gubi**

Sold in select stores around Europe, Gubi's products can be seamlessly combined to form integrated and intimate interiors in a wide variety of homes. Based in Copenhagen, Gubi works with both seasoned and up-and-coming international designers to produce collections that balance lightness and weight in an interplay of wiry metal lines and solid shapes. Generally muted in palette, Gubi knows how to carefully place pops of color — and how to intersperse elegant, simple items with quite unusual, complex pieces. One elegant home produce is the Bestline BL5, a lacquered and chromed steel wall lamp designed by Robert Dudley Best and produced by Gubi.

PP 503 THE CHAIR
Denmark
DESIGNER: **Hans J. Wegner**, PRODUCER: **PP Møbler**

Hans J. Wegner designed PP 503, "The Chair," in 1949, describing it as "the round one." The sleek, rounded armchair contributed to the international recognition of Danish design, making it the epitome of a historical moment and an ideal representative of Scandinavia's continuing influence on design around the world.

clockwise:

1 46 SOFA

2 FJ LAMP

3 CHIEFTAIN CHAIR
Denmark
DESIGNER: **Finn Juhl**, PRODUCER: **Onecollection**

Finn Juhl, born in 1912, was a Danish architect and interior and industrial designer best known for his furniture design. His beloved pieces like the Chieftan Chair, 46 Sofa, and FJ lamp, are notable for their soft-edged take on modernist design; Juhl favored organic shapes inspired by sculpture. The designer was one of the leading figures in Danish modern design, and was the person to successfully introduce the style to the United States. Today, Juhl's soft and elegant pieces are produced by Danish company Onecollection and adored by lovers of classic design around the world.

BASIC SERIES – WINE CARAFE and GLASS

Oslo, Norway

DESIGNER: **Frost Produkt with StokkeAustad**

Frost products are sturdy, durable, natural, and basic tools and accessories for the home. One clever group of pieces designed together with Norwegian design office StokkeAustad includes a water carafe, wine decanter, and old-fashioned glasses. These items belong to Frost's Basic Series, which are tools for the kitchen and dining table that emphasize comfort and usability.

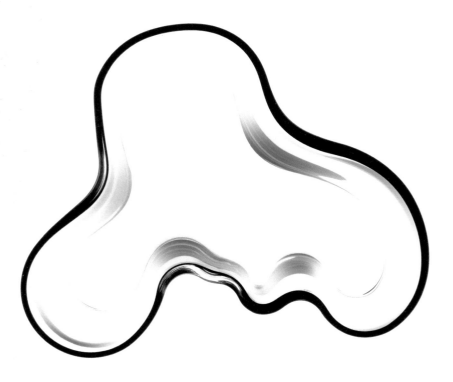

AALTO VASE

Iittala, Finland

DESIGNER: **Alvar Aalto**, PRODUCER: **Iittala**

Starting as a glass factory in Iittala, Finland in 1881, Iittala focuses on essential objects to enrich everyday life. Iittala's Aalto vase was designed by Alvar Aalto In 1936, and was first presented at the Paris World fair the following year. The glass vase's fluid, organic form is still mouth-blown today at the Iittala factory. It takes a team of seven skilled craftsment working together to create one Aalto vase, a uniquely crafted icon of modern design.

JOANNA LAAJISTO

Interior Architect | Helsinki, Finland

LAYERING OLD AND NEW IN FUNCTIONAL AESTHETICISM

For Joanna Laajisto, good design lasts a lifetime, both conceptually and physically. With a design philosophy driven by functionality and aesthetics, she seeks "not to clutter this world with unnecessary things but to find the hidden beauty of each space and to enhance it through creative solutions." Her spaces are often characterized by a blend of old and new, revealing layers of textures and colors in a harmonious unity.

The Helsinki-based interior architect studied and started her career on the West Coast of the United States. She received a B.A. from the prestigious Interior Design School of Southern California (IDI) in 2005, going on to work in Los Angeles at an international architectural firm designing large-scale commercial projects. During that time, she also received supplemental LEED* accreditation in green design. Since returning to her native Finland in 2008 to work as an independent interior architect, Laajisto has gained increasing attention for her growing portfolio that reflects her aesthetics of quiet emotionality.

You have designed a number of (semi) public spaces (offices, restaurants, retail spaces, etc.) and they all have a very personal, welcoming, relaxed feel. What are the key ingredients in creating such an atmosphere in a space?

I like to create public spaces that have an intimate, homey kind of feel. I use layers of old and new, mix design styles and

I think my designs speak about a certain kind of way of living (lifestyle) that can actually be found globally, not just in the Nordic countries. I respect the heritage of a space or an item and use that as a source of inspiration. What makes my design Nordic is that I like to use local materials, such as pine and oak wood. I also use lots of vintage items mixed with new design, and the pieces that are readily available here are mostly Scandinavian design classics.

I am drawn to a neutral color palette, sometimes warm, sometimes cold depending on the space. Neutrals create a timeless and calming background to a space. But I am not afraid to use pops of color as an accent. If color is used on large surfaces, such as walls or floors, I like to mute it down to soft pastels.

I guess I like a certain calmness or even melancholy in a space. Maybe that is a Scandinavian or more specifically Finnish quality. We are a quite melancholic people.

You mention that you like to combine new and old. Can you elaborate on this? What kinds of Scandinavian design items have you used and in what combination?

For example, I prefer to use vintage Alvar Aalto pieces to new ones. Old pieces of furniture from Artek have a wonderful patina and are much more interesting than the

> *"I use layers of old and new, mix design styles and like to use traditional elements in a new way. People feel relaxed when they are surrounded by familiar objects and when things are a bit worn down."*

like to use traditional elements in a new way. People feel relaxed when they are surrounded by familiar objects and when things are a bit worn down.

To what extent do you create a Scandinavian or Nordic atmosphere? A Finnish atmosphere?

newer models. The more scrapes, paint marks, and other flaws, the better.
For the meeting room at Sherpa advertising agency I used vintage Aalto 69 chairs in

(*note from the editor: LEED [Leadership in Energy and Environmental Design] is a certification system established by the U.S. Green Building Council and has become a standard in North America and internationally for measuring sustainability in the design, construction, and operation of high-performance green buildings.)

LEFT AND RIGHT PAGE:

For Bar & Co, Joanna Laajisto created four rooms with distinct atmospheres while maintaining coherency in design. The design combines classic bistro style elements with a contemporary twist. Custom wrought-iron fixtures, textile birds, and vintage copper accents add a sense of warmth and intimacy.

natural and black paired with a modern white table from Hay.

The TV armoire and table lamp were found in vintage shops. For the same project, modern Danish arm chairs were reupholstered in black wool fabric and paired with a comfortable modern sofa. Using vintage and new together gives the space interesting layers.

How did studying and working in the United States — and the West Coast in particular — influence your (Scandinavian) sense of aesthetics?

In Los Angeles I learned to respect design classics. There the architecture is very much influenced by mid-century modern design. But at the same time they don't have the burden of long history and traditions, so new architecture and design can be quite bold, contemporary, and inventive there.

I think that using both, the old and new, is what inspires me the most. I respect traditions but don't like to copy something that has already been done.

How would you describe classic Scandinavian design vs. the very contemporary? What are differences, what are similarities?

We Scandinavians are very proud of our heritage. Many designers, myself included, draw inspiration from the rich Scandinavian mythology and old traditional ways of doing things.

We are also very practical and think functionality even before aesthetics. Because of that, Nordic design can be very honest and that is why it appeals to many people.

In the United States you became a LEED-accredited interior architect. What aspects of your work reflect an environmentally sustainable approach?

In addition to using sustainable materials with low VOC (volatile organic compound) content, I like to design things that will last more then a passing trend. I hope that my

THIS PAGE (CLOCKWISE):

1 Laajisto created a familiar, small apartment atmosphere for the Gulled furniture showroom, featuring a table and chairs from Hay, Tom Dixon's iconic copper shade lamp, and a rolling file cabinet and stepladder by Magis.
2 An interior Joanna designed for the Sherpa Agency, an advertising agency in Helsinki.
3 Detail from an interior Joanna designed for Pinata, an animation and illustration studio in Helsinki.

designs will last over 10, 20, or 50 years both conceptually and physically. I think that is what makes design good.

What would you like to design but have not yet had a chance to do?

I am hoping that I will get a change to design an intimate boutique hotel with a restaurant-bar where the local crowd can mix with visiting tourists.
    I am also crazy about lighting and have already designed some one-off pieces for my projects. But in the future I would love to work with a lighting manufacturer and design a range of light fixtures.

A look into the home of Joanna Laajisto and Mikko Ryhänen. The apartment from 1928 was initially very dark, but after extensive renovation, they transformed it into a light and comfortable oasis to weather the dark winter. Mikko and Joanna used wooden vintage pieces, color accents from textiles and art, and warm metal accents to add a bit of sparkle. Modern classics such as Bertoia dining chairs and a Platner coffee table are items that Joanna and Mikko wish to pass on to their children.

EXTRA LIGHT

Stepping into a big open space, the white floors spread out before you and the big windows surrounding the building on all sides let the light flow freely. Your eyes are drawn to the big sofa placed in the middle of the room like a sculpture or art installation. There isn't much more in the room, just a pile of books and a few cushions on the concrete bench beside the fireplace. On the wall, the star of the room: a huge abstract painting in strong colors. As you walk into the kitchen you are met by stainless steel counters, butcher-style tiles from floor to ceiling, and on the table a simple candle holder.

Behind the kitchen is an entrance to the more private areas of the house, where the serene atmosphere continues in bedrooms and bathrooms by keeping the materials simple, the surfaces clear, and the furnishings spare.

Minimalist, or functionalist, the border between these movements is a bit blurred, but what they both agree on is that all your belongings should be useful and have a purpose other than their beauty. According to the minimalists, simplifying your home also means simplifying your life, as you will no longer have to spend time looking for your belongings. The few items you have will be neatly organized instead of buried under piles of other things. At the same time, cleaning becomes much easier, as your surfaces will be mostly empty, except for perhaps a bowl or lamp.

Materialwise, this style uses natural materials such as stone, wood, concrete, and glass for the structure of the building, both inside and out, and decorates with steel and laminated furniture, keeping upholstered furniture to a minimum. A bit of softness is instead added with a few plants, some interesting art, and strategic lighting. But most of all, the color and life in the house are meant to come from its inhabitants.

FOUR-CORNERED VILLA
Virrat, Finland

ARCHITECT: **Avanto Architects**, PHOTOGRAPHER: **Anders Portman and Martin Sommerschield**

The site of Avanto Architects' Four-cornered Villa is a horseshoe-shaped island in the Finnish countryside that faces northeast. Defined yet open and airy, the villa is a carbon-neutral home — in contrast to typical Finnish cottages, which waste energy on heating. Here the electricity is powered by solar energy, and the sun also provides generous light at all times of day. Like all projects by Avanto Architects, Four-cornered Villa is the result of an equal collaboration between partners Ville Hara and Anu Puustine. The Helsinki-based office offers both planning and design services, including projects of varying scale for a wide range of public and private clients.

KYMMENDÖ SUMMER HOUSE

Stockholm Archipelago, Sweden
ARCHITECT: **Jordens Arkitekter**, PHOTOGRAPHER: **Åke E:son Lindman**

Nestled on a thin strip of land in the Stockholm archipelago, the Kymmendö house was designed by Jordens Arkiteker to be as hidden as possible within the landscape. Its "cigar box" interior is finely crafted in warm woods, and all rooms face the scenery with only sliding glass partitions as a thin separation between indoors and outdoors. A supporting concrete basement grounds Kymmendö solidly in the island rock, topped with a wooden deck that supports the house's above-ground steel frame. A cantilevered wood-beam roof is an aesthetically streamlined cap to the home's minimal and natural design.

BLOMKVIST APARTMENT

Stockholm, Sweden
ARCHITECT: **Bunker Hill**

With clean lines and a deceptively simple use of space, Daniel Franzén often creates interiors that feel big despite remarkably small floor plans — including one of the smallest apartments in Stockholm at only 11 square meters. With a sparing selection of light furniture, lofted spaces, light woods like pine plywood and MDF, and daring wall cutouts, Franzén creates luxurious apartments and homes of any size. Founded in 2005, his office, Bunker Hill, is based in Sollentuna, Sweden.

BLOMKVIST APARTMENT

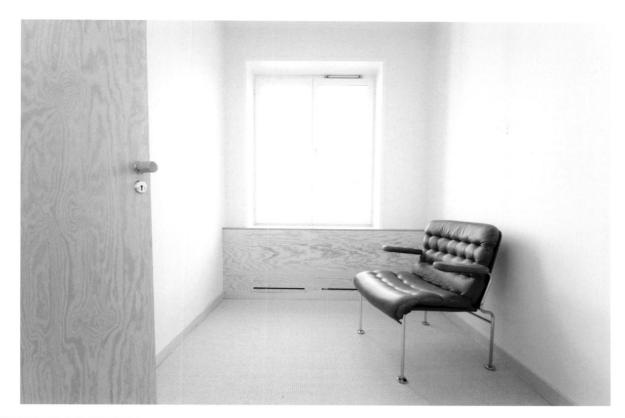

SUMMERHOUSE SKÅNE
Österlen, Sweden
ARCHITECT: **LASC Studio**, PHOTOGRAPHER: **Thomas Ibsen, Stamers Kontor**

The first project completed as the product of the collaboration between Jonas Labbé & Johannes Schotanus of LASC Studio, Summerhouse Skåne is a converted farmhouse in the Swedish countryside. Opening up the plan of traditional dark farmhouses by inserting large garden-facing windows, and removing two-thirds of the interior walls and ceilings, the space has been reinterpreted for contemporary life. With surprising orange and turquoise accents, this lovely project clearly displays LASC's signature understated yet playful use of color.

SUMMERHOUSE SKÅNE

CITY COTTAGE

Helsinki, Finland

ARCHITECT: **Verstas Architects**, PHOTOGRAPHER: **Andreas Meichsner**

Finns love to spend time in nature — even when it's nestled in the middle of a city. This 14-square-meter vacation getaway in Helsinki's city center is only two kilometers from the home of its family of four. Its proximity to home means that the cottage doesn't need to be stocked with necessities year-round, making it an ecological solution to the problem of long-distance vacations, extra belongings, and large houses. When designing the home, Verstas architects considered the efficient spatial arrangements of boats and caravans to organize a fully functional interior that sleeps four and allows multiple uses of every room. The cottage is in development for serial production by Verstas in collaboration with Finnish wooden house manufacturer Finnlamelli.

NANNBERGA SUMMER HOUSE

Nannberga, Arboga, Sweden
ARCHITECT: **General Architecture**, PHOTOGRAPHER: **Mikael Olsson**

To construct the Nannberga Summer House, General Architecture moved an existing timber structure to the home's site in Nanberga, Sweden, where it was placed on in situ concrete walls. The wooden frame heightens the structure to create two full floors, the second of which is divided by two load-bearing walls that span between the perimeter walls and leave the ground floor open. The geometric grid in which the house is inscribed informs the positions of its walls, windows, and doors. The Stockholm-based practice stuck to straightforward and efficient building methods in line with the trajectory of today's best Nordic design.

THE CABIN W35
Drøbak, Oslo Fjord
DESIGNER: **Marianne Borge**, PHOTOGRAPHER: **Ivan Brodey**

Durable, sustainable design was the starting point for the creation
of Woody35. As its name suggests, this home near the Oslo Fjord
is a space-efficient 35-square-meter cabin built from mainte-
nance-free wood. Designer Marianne Borge emphasized natural
light and preserved unobstructed contact between the indoors and
outdoors, enhanced by sliding glass doors allowing both light and
a view. The living room's double height has a feeling of generous
space, complete with a fireplace and a lofted bedroom above. All
products within the home were selected with a focus on sustainable solutions.

THE CABIN W35

THE DUNE HOUSE
Suffolk, UK
ARCHITECT: **Jarmund / Vigsnæs AS Architects MNAL**

The Dune House is a holiday rental house that brings stunning Scandinavian design all the way to England's Suffolk Coast. Designed by Oslo-based architecture office JVA, the house is part of the Living Architecture Initiative, an enterprise that invites world-class architects to design homes around Britain for anyone to rent — to experience living, eating, and sleeping in an outstanding architectural space.

When designing this house nestled into coastal dunes, JVA took care to relate its external appearance to the existing strip of typical British seaside houses nearby. This sensitivity led to a contrasting appearance between the building's upper and lower floors, an architectural ambiguity that also appropriately address the programmatic differences between the spaces: private above, social below.

THE DUNE HOUSE

LOKSTALLET
Gotland, Hablingbo, Sweden
INTERIOR STYLIST: **Sofie Ganeva**, CLIENT: **Fantastic Frank**,
PHOTOGRAPHER: **Kristofer Johnson**

Fantastic Frank is a Stockholm-based real estate office that markets homes so comfortable and flexible their clients will never want to leave. Recreating both houses and hotels, Sofie Ganeva for Fantastic Frank provides a fresh, modern aesthetic while remaining true to a building's history. Pictured here, Ganeva decked out the Lokstallat house in Gotland, Sweden, which was once a locomotive repair and storage barn — and is now a trendy summer home for a Stockholm family. The residence is hospitable yet retains an industrial feel, indicative of Fantastic Frank's eclectic style and creative approach.

TOMAS BACKMAN

Creative Director & Partner, FANTASTIC FRANK | Stockholm, Sweden

NEXT GENERATION BROKERS MAKE EVERY HOME A DESIGN GEM

You don't always want to judge a book by its cover, but in some businesses, it could make or break the bank. Take real estate. In Stockholm, Fantastic Frank has raised the bar in real estate brokerage. Their philosophy is to treat every property they represent like a Sleeping Beauty: "We're not interested in creating something that the majority of buyers are going to like. We're interested in creating something that at least one person is going to positively LOVE because at the end of the day, a house or apartment can only have one owner. Our job therefore, is to find that one person and seduce them!"

To that end, since their founding in 2010, Fantastic Frank has worked with a rotating roster of talented photographers and stylists from fashion, design, and architecture, creating high-gloss images of their properties that wouldn't seem out of place in the best interior design magazines.

In fact, many have been featured there, as the brokerage makes international headlines for their forward-thinking approach to the industry. Comprehensive market coverage occurs through blogs, tweets, social networking, and more. An internet reality TV series is planning to follow the Fantastic Frank team as

they style and sell their properties throughout Stockholm and possibly beyond: a satellite office in Berlin is scheduled to open in the summer of 2013.

Please describe what makes Fantastic Frank unique as a real estate agent. How do you work?

Fantastic Frank uses interior stylists for every property we sell. On top of that,

Fantastic Frank was founded by Tomas Backman, Mattias Kardell, and Sven Wallén. We noticed that there was a gap in the market: there were no real estate agents who seemed to be interested in aesthetics. All the agents we encountered had similar approaches. We created Fantastic Frank to have a "design position" on the market.

All three founders have a genuine interest in beautiful design and architecture. We are all Stockholmers and as such are very picky about everything we buy for our homes, clothes, where we eat, and so on. Stockholmers are very, very aware of their own image. They also identify strongly with where they live.

In such a culture, there was and is a crystal clear need for a real estate agent that radiates the big city lifestyle, who takes care of the properties in the same manner as the fashion and interior design industry does. We saw this first as a business opportunity. But we knew that we had to make a product with our hearts — a product that we ourselves would want to use.

Clearly the properties you represent are truly "fantastic" once you are finished with them. But what is the idea behind "Frank"?

The other real estate agents have such dull names you never remember them. I wanted a name that was catchy. "Frank" is by coincidence — and my first son's middle name.

"We make them feel even prouder of their homes. We give them a brochure of the best quality with images of their home at its prime."

we use photographers from the fashion, advertising, and architecture. This also makes a huge difference since we produce photographs suited for interior magazines. In our branch, this is totally unique. In some countries, agents still take their own photos.

Who are the founders and how did they come together to form this company?

In your projects you seem to be creating the perfect atmosphere for the Scandinavian market. Can you identify some of the key elements that "work" for your properties?

We don't have a fixed formula for what we do. We just produce exciting and beautiful images to showcase the particular living space. We can do this because our staff of

stylists and photographers are given enough time for their work — and don't work on a conveyor belt. For the interiors, we start with the things we find in the homes we sell — and then add a few borrowed items here and there as seems fit. We never try to force a home into being something that it's not.

What we have to do, each time, is to identify the target group — who might buy the property — and then design the property to attract that audience. Sometimes we take into account the image of the neighborhood the home is in and make reference to that in the styling.

Who are your clients? What defines their taste?

Our clients are Stockholmers — picky Stockholmers! If you live in Stockholm you are automatically picky and trend-sensitive! At first, we thought we would only have design collectors, but we have all sorts of clients and that makes our job so much more fun!

LEFT AND RIGHT PAGE:

The industrial feel of a former locomotive house was complemented by the warm colors of antique furniture and carpets for a balanced contrast appealing to style-savvy Stockholmers looking for a summer home.

LEFT AND RIGHT PAGE:

A former railway warehouse was for sale as a hotel or large multifamily vacation house. Fantastic Frank styled it to attract both categories of buyers. Original details were highlighted — revealed beams, masonry walls, and typical Gotland sandstone — and paired with handpicked vintage furniture for a familiar, authentic atmosphere.

You put a lot of care into the properties. What goes into your care of the people?

We make them feel even prouder of their homes. We give them a brochure of the best quality with images of their home at its prime.

What characteristics do you look for in a property to represent?

We basically sell anything, but it seems that the only people who contact us are proud of their homes, so we have hardly had any ugly properties to sell so far. When we take on a property, we look for its character — whatever that character may be. The most difficult properties are newly built apartments with a total lack of soul and life. Still, we find each and every property unique — our mission is to highlight the beauty of it. And it works.

VILLA WIENBERG

Højbjerg, Denmark
ARCHITECT: **Wienberg Arkitekter**, PHOTOGRAPHER: **Mikkel Rahr Mortensen**

This intimate Danish summerhouse, designed by Mette and Martin Wienberg, is a rigorous play of light, material, and volume. The design is simple and abstract: hard lines of concrete and steel are tempered by the warmth of wood and softened by leather and fur, white curtains, large windows, and soft lighting. The result is the effect of a "warm cove," both functional and comfortable, in which every family member can find his or her own space. Furniture from Arper lends personality and sophistication to the rooms — in which views of the garden are framed like paintings.

Dinesen's exclusive HeartOak planks are solid boards with widths up to half a meter and lengths up to six meters. The planks come from the center of giant, ancient oaks, using as much of the wood as possible in appreciation for these specially selected trees, which in this case may be up to two centuries old.

LOKAL

Helsinki, Finland
PHOTOGRAPHER: **Katja Hagelstam**

Katja Hagelstam is a freelance photographer whose specialties are antiques, interiors, and food. Living in Laajasalo, a neighborhood of islands in Southern Helsinki, she seeks intimate arrangements of objects and special furniture items to compose images according to a uniquely Finnish sensibility. Hagelstam has recently opened Lokal, a new concept gallery in Helsinki that showcases contemporary Finnish art, craft, and design.

UMAMI SANTOKU

Voss, Norway
DESIGNER: **Per Finne**

Per Finne's Umami Santoku knives are designed to feel like an extension of the hand. With a perfectly smooth transition between handle and blade, it can be gripped in a variety of ways for versatile use. The knife's blade is forged steel and its handle is oak, connected with a single oak peg. Umami Santoku comes housed in a wooden box conformed to its graceful outline.

HOUSE MORRAN
Gothenburg Archipelago, Sweden
ARCHITECT: **Johannes Norlander Arkitektur AB**

On an island near the sea fairway leading to the port of Gothenburg, Johannes Norlander Arkitektur transformed a worn-down cottage from the 1950s with an extension from the 1970s into a livable, beautiful home for today. The structure was kept mostly intact in order not to waste new materials, but was reinforced and refined to bring out the existing qualities of the site. The architects installed a new façade of plywood coated in black pine tar, which mimics the traditional process of preserving wooden boats, and a simple tar-paper roof with thin plywood eaves and aluminum gutters tops the house. The stark interior architecture is kept visible and bare, clad entirely in natural pine.

actuele architectuur
topical architecture
architecture actuelle
aktuell Architektur

VILLA MECKLIN
Mustaluoto, Velkua, Naantali, Finland
ARCHITECT: **Huttunen–Lipasti–Pakkanen Architects**

Villa Mecklin was designed primarily on-site: the architects at Huttunen–Lipasti–Pakkanen spent plenty of time over a four-year span scouting out the villa's location in the Finnish archipelago, a difficult terrain for anyone to build on. Contract documents and working drawings were not necessary for the completion of this angular, natural-wood house, as all practical issues were resolved on-site. Its sheltered terrace extends over the summit of the rock upon which it rests, providing a stunning view from outside. On the grounds the villa includes a shoreline sauna and stove-heated cabin for guests.

THE TRIANGLE HOUSE
Nesodden, Norway
ARCHITECT: **Jarmund / Vigsnæs AS Architects MNAL**

On a rocky hillside facing the sea in Nesodden, Norway, sits this angular residence designed by JVA. With its back to a pine forest, the three-story, 286-square-meter home has an exterior of dark wood panels and a raw-looking interior clad with wooden OSB boards. The floors are cast in concrete and partly covered with sisal mats, and the maximized layout is punctuated by expansive windowpanes. Despite strict building guidelines, the Norwegian architects constructed a unique space expressing a duality between angularity and flow — a design whose success can be measured by the fact that its inhabitants claim to sleep very soundly inside their home.

MIRKKU KULLBERG

Managing Director, ARTEK | Helsinki, Finland

SUSTAINABLE SPIRIT TAKES DESIGN MASTER INTO THE FUTURE

Artek has shaped Scandinavian design aesthetics for nearly 80 years, having filled everything from public spaces to homes, museums, schools, hotels, and offices. The Finnish company was founded in 1935 by Alvar and Aino Aalto, Maire Gullichsen, and Nils-Gustav Hahl "to sell furniture and to promote modern culture of habitation by exhibitions and other means."

Its name reveals the founders' forward thinking and their desire to unite art with technology in their work. Aalto's methods for bending and splicing wood to realize the organic, sculptural forms of his furniture designs were revolutionary in the 1930s and went on to be a hallmark of his work. The clear lines and functionalism of his creations, married with the warmth of wood and other natural materials, gave them a timelessness and appeal that persists to this day.

While sustainability as a word was not always part of the company vernacular, its spirit was always at the core of Artek. An emphasis on high quality and longevity, along with the economic use of local materials, are criteria upheld by advocates and practitioners of sustainable design today. The notion of sustainability as durability in the widest sense was taken a step further in 2007 by Managing Director Mirkku Kullberg and Creative Director Tom Dixon, with the bold 2nd Cycle program, through which the company buys back used Artek stools and chairs for resale.
    While the renewal and reissue of Aalto's designs are a cornerstone of the business, Artek is eagerly moving forward to collaborate with select designers, architects, and artists on new works and projects, to explore the use of new materials, and to develop new standards and technologies that reflect and maintain the company's original spirit.

How would you describe the current state of Scandinavian design?

Scandinavian design is very much influenced by the waves and the look of the international design scene. Designers and ideas do not have any borders and not really any homeland either. I do not want to be cynical, but the time we are living in needs design idealism and more bold movements. Or does it, if consumers are happy with all hybrids and designs for the sake of design … ? Think about the amount of design objects shown in Milan, for example. The exhibition is full of chairs, stools, and objects that live only for their time at the fair and a few weeks after without any hope of production kick-off, or a few months if the press has praised them, or some years only because some courageous souls believe in the potential of the ideas behind them.

Do not understand me wrong: I am an optimist. I like the niche of Scandinavian design, where you can still see the touch of arts

Crisis brings better ideas and innovations, leading us to make emotionally and rationally better products.
    In general, there is too much and too average design in the world. We need pioneers and heroes. Designers need companies to commit and designers need to challenge themselves.

How does Artek fit into the picture, as an iconic brand with a legacy reaching back more than 70 years?

The company Artek was founded in 1935 by four deeply talented persons with radical thoughts. They wanted to educate consumers by showing a new vision of beauty and a new approach to local materials, by thinking out of the box with regard to production, and to combine art and technology, like the name "Artek" states. I think Artek was a movement that gathered a kind of tribe around it. It was a Nordic Bauhaus utopia with a humanistic touch.
    Artek feels very relevant today and we have been able, after quite a stagnant period, to bring back an uncompromising sprit. At Artek we believe that we can have an impact on design consumption.
    We believe that we can oppose the average, praise the authentic, and avoid the consensus. This is very much about having courage, finding the right competence for the company, and creating new generation communities.

> *"I think Artek was a movement that gathered a kind of tribe around it. It was a Nordic Bauhaus utopia with humanistic touch."*

and crafts and the purpose of design is very much about function and everyday needs. Simple and easy things are coming back. I think there is a great momentum for Scandinavian design and we should play our cards right. This time of insecurity, with economic, ethical, and environmental changes, is creating a conservative market and consumers are critical. People want to make sensible decisions and to consume with attitude.

What are the key ingredients for an Artek product/project?

The key ingredients for an Artek product or project are: time, time, and time. Good products and ideas are born from processes. Masters, like technical experts, need to have time to work together with the designers, to find the right language — and then comes the dialogue.

THIS PAGE (CLOCKWISE):

1 Chairs 65 and 66, designed by Alvar Aalto, 1935. WHITE Collection lamps by Ville Kokkonen, 2010.
2 Pirkka Table and Bench, designed by Ilmari Tapiovaara, 1955.
3 Table 81B and Chair 69, designed by Alvar Aalto, 1935.

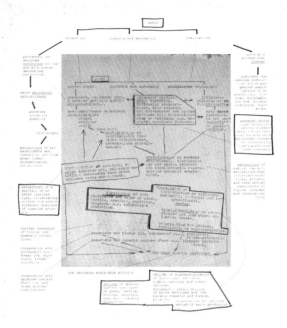

Then there is: work, work, and work. We need to be ready to work hard and find the right mixture of passion and ambition. Risks must be taken and mistakes must be allowed because they are the paths to new and innovative fields.

Finally, commitment is needed from the companies to wait for the best results.

Can you talk a bit about the Artek manifesto, how the company started, and what its foundations are?

Artek's founding manifesto is the best-ever written business manual, brand manual, and road map for any kind of company. It is simultaneously an art of words, language, system theory, activity plan, propaganda statement, and educational pamphlet.

Artek's founders wrote a one-page manual for the company: a founding letter that explains how to combine art and technology. At the center of that chart were Alvar Aalto's design products, created through architectural processes. Products were manufactured with standards and systems in industrial processes. That was technology! Its founders saw art like education and a way of creating a special ambiance, and colors should support the holistic approach of beauty. Art was a communication tool and way of making tribes and communities.

The manifesto called for propaganda, not PR or communication. It was heavyweight, intelligent, radical, and progressive thinking. That was the social media, that was the recommendation in marketing; that was so cool.

After I read the manifesto for the first time, I decided not to talk anymore about brands or trends. Even words like "public relations" felt really light....

How do you handle the interconnection between heritage and innovation? What are the most interesting challenges?

Heritage can be a benefit or a burden, and that is the challenge we need to understand. All products introduced and launched will be compared to the existing iconic pieces by Aalto. But that should inspire people to think better and wider. We implement thinking boldly. Our heritage is interesting, but we do not need to copy our existing products. We need to move the company forward and think about the world tomorrow.

We think that there needs to be the same level of values behind the new innovation as with the heritage pieces.

Our heritage creates the trust that our processes are needed and gives the management the confidence to take risks and allow mistakes.

Aalto's pieces had a deep connection to interiors and architecture. This is a motivation

for our new design as well. We make studies of the future libraries, retirement homes, and hospitality areas. This is to understand the world of the next generation.

For us, innovation is driven by need; for other companies the driving factor might be the desire industry. But need was the driver in the past for Artek and continues to be so now.

Please explain the idea behind Artek's 2nd Cycle Project.

Artek 2nd Cycle was a manifesto against the madness of Milan 2007 and the fair buzz in general: the press, dealers, and consumers were running after newness and the latest of the latest. Artek had been blamed often for showing the "old" Aalto icons and nothing new.

Our question was: so what if we think that old is better than most of the new things out there? In 2007, the word "sustainability" was quite new, while the whole design scene was dancing tango with fashion — fast and furious. Artek wanted to challenge the whole scene and declared Sustainability as Attitude and started talking about authenticity and origin of the design. We wanted also to talk about quality and design as an investment. Artek is the only company that can really own the second-hand

market as we still have the same production, same standards, and systems with product components.

The main idea behind 2nd Cycle is to talk about longevity and durability — the main factors when talking about sustainability. Our motto is "One Chair is Enough," meaning that the Artek product can live from one generation to the next one without losing its value or identity. The design, the beauty, and the quality stand for time. We also think that people need layers in their lives. 2nd Cycle is an excellent way of combining the old and the new. This gives people wider perspectives.

What is the directive of design in the world today?

The directive of design today is the same as it was before. The changing world needs good products enabling people to improve the quality of their lives. Design is and should be part of everyday life, and it should

"In general, there is too much and too average design in the world. We need pioneers and heroes. Designers need companies to commit and designers need to challenge themselves."

be educative and inspiring. Good design should create an experience for all senses. Less is not always more, and regardless of whether it is more or less — it should be aiming for better!

LEFT PAGE:

1 The original Artek Manifesto, drawn up when the company was founded in 1935 by Alvar and Aino Aalto, Maire Gullichsen, and Nils-Gustav Hahl.
2 Vintage Stool 60s acquired through the Artek 2nd Cycle program, established in 2007.

THIS PAGE:

1 The Artek factory in Turku, Finland, where Alvar Aalto's original designs from the 1930s are still produced today.
2 To celebrate the 80th birthday of Alvar Aalto's iconic Stool 60, designer Nao Tamura created Ring, a limited edition version of the stool featuring a graphic depiction of tree rings lacquered onto the seat.

DINESEN DOUGLAS
Rødding, Denmark
ARCHITECT: **Wingårdh Arkitektkontor and**
Therkildsen Arkitekter, PRODUCER: **Dinesen**

Founded in 1898 by the same family that runs the company today, Dinesen has never abandoned the age-old craftsmanship that makes their outstanding wooden floors so recognizable. From homes to castles to museums to churches, Dinesen's meticulously selected and prepared wooden planks can be found in buildings around the world. Favored for their unusually large size, the boards are installed in a way that renders partitions and joints invisible, and they are sure to stand the test of time — after all, Dinesen's wood comes from trees between 80 and 100 years old.

VEDBÆK HOUSE

Vedbæk, Denmark

ARCHITECT: **Norm Architects**, PHOTOGRAPHER: **Jonas Bjerre-Poulsen**

The first thing Norm Architects did when building the Vedbæk House was to tear down all the walls, leaving only the chimney in place and opening up the entire ground floor into one big room. This allowed the beautiful old staircase leading to the upper floor to be prominently featured. All the floors, walls, and ceilings of this cozy home on the Danish coast are painted white, connecting all spaces visually regardless of their architectural differences and reflecting light to create the illusion of a larger space. Below the house is a rustic, 100-year-old wine cellar.

HOME of JAKOB NYLUND and MIA WALLMARK

Stockholm, Sweden
DESIGNER: **Jakob Nylund and Mia Wallmark**

When designing their own home, Jakob Nylund and Mia Wallmark wanted to create an interior that was both masculine and feminine, black and white, cold and warm. Because having friends over for dinner is one of the couple's favorite activities, the centerpiece of their redesigned apartment is a wooden table made from 120-year-old floorboards, created by a friend. Around the table are six different chairs, including classics like the Eames Eiffel chair and the Bertola wire chair, as well as more modern items like the Chair One. The whole interior is full of personal touches, handmade items, and creative lighting solutions.

CORNER APARTMENT
No. 2

No. 1

CORNER APARTMENT
No. 1 and 2

Stockholm, Sweden
ARCHITECT: **Guise**, PHOTOGRAPHER: **Pierre Bibby and
Jesper Lindström**

Swedish interior designers Guise often experiment with the concept of the void. By installing dark spaces in what might seem like
a counterintuitive approach, they have found ingenious ways to
create the illusion of expanded space.
In one Stockholm apartment, Janni Kristoffersen and Andreas
Ferm from Guise reconceived the home of a client working in
the fashion industry who needed a larger-seeming space for
his fashion-related books and items. Applying black shapes and
installing a custom kitchen, the designers were able to conceal
the depth of the space — in their words: "the only limit is your own
imagination."

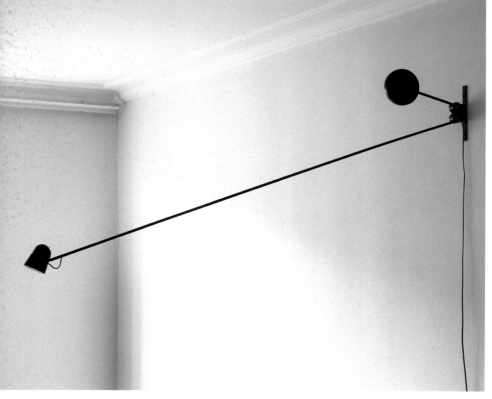

clockwise:

1 RICOCHET LIGHT
2 COHERENCE LIGHT
3 COUNTERBALANCE
Oslo, Norway
DESIGNER: **Daniel Rybakken**, PRODUCER: **Spazio Rossana Orlandi**

Daniel Rybakken has reinvented the lamp — many times. His creative use of reflection and ability to delicately balance many components create expressive, conceptually complex, and useful lighting solutions. For example, a gravity-defying lamp called Counterbalance relies on a system of cogwheels and gears to illuminate an entire space, creating a strong graphic impression. Other projects, such as the Ricochet lamp, exploit mirrors to create surprising, shifting reflections. The young Norwegian designer frames his projects as "experiments," always seeking new ways to simplify or expand upon basic design concepts.

RAW EDGES

A birch tree rises to the ceiling, an unexpected indoor feature, but totally in tune with the rest of this home. You put your teacup down on a tree stump beside you, leaning back onto the soft sheepskin covering your corner of the couch. Letting your feet rest on the table made from old pallets, you look up at the big industrial pendant lights, wondering what they might have been through, what kind of factory they used to hang in. Many of the items around you seem to have lived another life before landing here; some come from the forests and beaches in the area and some from more industrial places like factories or railway stations. However, they all seem to coexist peacefully now, creating a whole that is rustic, harmonious, and comfortable.

Nature finds mixed with folk art and industrial pieces, those are words that neatly sum up the rustic style. Everything has a history, but is kept fresh by combining this with a color range that stretches from milky white to espresso, with some rust, gray, and black thrown into the mix as well. Aside from the occasional stripe or folklore flower, patterns are mainly avoided in favor of interesting textures like longhaired sheepskins, rough crinkled linen, or rusty metal. The materials used are of course completely natural; plastic is banned here and replaced with porcelain, concrete, rubber, glass, and cork. Woods in all colors and varieties are also used generously, not only for floors and furniture but also for ceilings and walls. Decorations are mainly brought in from nature and can be a tray with a collection of seashells from the summer, or pinecones and autumn leaves when the days are getting colder.

For a more industrial look, pipes and old bolts can be used for many purposes, like clothes hangers, candle holders, or lamps.

NAUST PAA AURE

Aure Kommune, Møre og Romsdal, Norway
ARCHITECT: **TYIN tegnestue Architects**

Norwegian boathouses were traditionally used for storing boats and fishing gear, but today many of them are converted for recreational summertime use. TYIN tegnestue Architects rebuilt one such boathouse dating back to the middle of the eighteenth century that sat dilapidated on the outermost reaches of Norway's Møre Coast. The structure was in such bad condition that it was torn down and built anew, with the simplicity, materiality, and placement of the original structure retained. The low-maintenance treatment of the Norwegian pine cladding, cotton canvas surfaces, and a sturdy steel roof all ensure that the boathouse, while relaxed and simple, will stand the test of time — remaining true to Norwegian historical and cultural heritage while catering to new use.

NAUST PAA AURE

ANDREAS G. GJERTSEN and YASHAR HANSTAD

Architects, TYIN TEGNESTUE ARCHITECTS | Norway

SUSTAINABLE ARCHITECTURE THROUGH ETHICS AND AESTHETICS

It all started out as a student project. In their third year at NTNU architecture school in Trondheim, Andreas G. Gjertsen and Yashar Hanstad traveled abroad to work on an orphanage project in Thailand, where they realized that they wanted to make high-quality architecture for "clients who actually benefit from the work we do."

Since starting their company TYIN back home in Trondheim in 2007, the architects have gone on to realize projects in Thailand, Uganda, and Indonesia, not to mention in their native Norway. They were recognized for their efforts in 2012 with the European Prize for Architecture, presented by the Chicago Athenaeum and the European Centre for Architecture Art Design and Urban Studies, honoring "rare architects who have demonstrated a significant contribution to humanity and to the built environment through the art of architecture."

TYIN emphasizes that they are not "humanitarian architects" but "building architects," and that their overall approach, which includes active dialogue with the client, working with the vernacular architecture, and willingly adapting to new challenges, can be applied everywhere. According to Gjertsen: "We practice local architecture that becomes internationally relevant, based on functional needs. And we want everything to look good too so we add this aesthetic functionality."

Scandinavians seem to have a particular relationship to the environment and nature around them. How would you describe that relationship for yourselves and your clients?

We live very close to nature in all of Norway. We have all kinds of weather during the year, and this becomes a big part of our everyday lives and over time it seeps into our culture. We are interested in the complex and the extreme. For us, the site and its environment is one of the most complex and extreme aspects of all our projects. This affects the way we work, and in the end this affects the architecture itself.

To be sensitive and humble to the situation you are working in is crucial if you want to discover architecture.

There is a Nordic tradition of having summer homes, second homes, and cabins. What are the key ingredients for such a place?

The usual cabin in Norway is not too far from your permanent residence. It is often in a different kind of environment (if you live in a costal city, your summer home is in the mountains and vice versa.) and many prefer a simple life in the holiday homes. Often the cabins lack electricity and water. This also shifts the daily routine and adds richness to life, which appeals to many Norwegians. Nostalgia also plays a large role in cabin culture.

In your work, what is the role of the (natural) materials you use (wood, stone, etc.)? What is the relevance of light and color?

We are drawn towards architecture that is understandable yet complex. Natural materials give us a lot in this sense. They are a bit unpredictable and have a will of their own. In the development of architecture, we believe in the value of curiosity and discovery over making up clever ideas and concepts. Natural materials like stone and wood give a wonderful kind of resistance that leads to a richer architecture that relates to the human being in a good way.

What are your own private places like? Would you say they have a particular Scandinavian touch?

One of the partners of TYIN lives in a 400-year-old timber log house in the forest outside Trondheim and another lives in a boat on the river running through the city.

LEFT PAGE:

Built for orphans living along the Thai-Burmese border, the "Butterfly Houses" (2008–2009) feature a façade of local woven bamboo and a unique roof providing natural ventilation and rainwater collection.

THIS PAGE:

For a Norwegian client, TYIN rebuilt an old boathouse (2010–2011), recycling some of its 150-year-old materials for internal use and adding windows salvaged from a nearby farmhouse.

This is probably due to a curiosity for architecture and alternative ways of living, and to acquire a sense of our personal limits.

What is the story behind your firm as well as its name, TYIN?

In 2007 the founding partners of TYIN bought a boat called TYIN and lived in it for a year before departing for the first projects in Thailand. The 110-year-old boat was first used as a tourist boat in Jotunheimen, a mountainous region in the middle of Norway. From 1906, the boat transported people on Lake Tyin for a hotel that was called Tyin Høyfjellshotell.

The name was naturally transferred to the company, since it inspired the first projects. Furthermore, the Norwegian word *tyin* can be roughly translated as "to go inside" or "to seek shelter." The more we developed our first few projects, this connection began to make more and more sense...

You have done a lot of work in Asia and Africa. How has your Nordic design sensibility been influenced by the situations in these countries? Are there parallels between the Asian and African sense of space and form you encountered and the Scandinavian design aesthetic?

There is a positive aspect to being foreign in many situations. The combination of research about the local culture and climate, combined with a new set of eyes, can often lead to new solutions that are strangely efficient.

In many ways we think that foreign cultures have affected us more than the other way around. Confronting their challenges

and situations has developed us as architects to a large extent.

The most basic human needs are universal all over the world, and the vernacular architecture we have seen is all closely related. There is a strange "us and them" flair to many of the questions we get about working outside Norway. We have tried to focus on being architects firstly and understanding what we can do as professionals. The challenges are usually based on the same mechanisms, and our most important tool is our methods.

Extreme situations, for example, characterize our work at home and abroad. We have encountered heat in Asia and Africa, and cold in Norway. Both climates require special attention to detailing and a sensitivity to how architecture solves these issues. In Asia and Africa, the social aspects of the processes are very complex, whereas in Norway the bureaucratic issues are very complex. This calls for architects that understand how to work with the flow and adapt to constantly new challenges and changes. Every situation calls for different solutions, but the process to understand and approach the situation doesn't change that much, in our view.

Please complete the sentence: the directive of architecture is to…

Like Juhani Pallasma once said: "Architecture is about the understanding of the world — and turning it into a more meaningful and humane place." Couldn't have said it better ourselves...

What are your next planned projects?

We are currently involved in a building project in Norway for an extension of a family house. The twist is that we are following up closely during the construction process, and have taken full control over the budget, contractors, and the construction process, as well. We believe that gaining better insight into the entire building process leads to a better result in the end.

We are also working on several small-scale projects in Norway and continue to take part in exhibitions and workshops in several countries. We are trying to find a good balance of working on our home turf and keeping connected to the different social and professional communities around the world.

KRÅKMORA HOLMAR

Archipelago outside Stockholm, Sweden
ARCHITECT: **Claesson Koivisto Rune**, PHOTOGRAPHER: **Åke E:son Lindman**

Claesson Koivisto Rune built this little summer cottage on an island in Stockholm's surrounding archipelago. The clients of Kråkmora Holmar vacation house were a family with two young children, who required both an efficient use of this 45-square-meter space and an efficient use of energy. With a strong geometric concept and careful selection of materials, the architects designed a vacation home that is both comfortable, bright, and sensitive to the environment — with a carefully insulated interior, stove heating, a composting toilet, and use of local materials. The yellow pine wood exterior has quickly transformed to a stony gray that blends in seamlessly with the home's natural surroundings.

KRÅKMORA HOLMAR

NIDO

Sipoo, Finland
DESIGNER: **Robin Falck Design**

Robin Falck began designing the Nido house when he was 18 and felt like he needed a place of his own. After researching and sketching for a year, he determined that to build a house without a permit would restrict the space to 10 square meters — and decided to maximize the possibilities for such a small area. The house's asymmetrical structure is designed to let as much nature in as possible; as Falk says: "The less indoors I have the more I can enjoy nature and the things that are outside of the box."

GOOD MORNING MOKA POT

Oslo, Norway
DESIGNER: **Torbjørn Anderssen and Espen Voll**

Good Morning Moka Pot was made especially for Food Work, a project initiated by four Norwegian designers to be shown at Tokyo Design Tide 2012. Moka Pot is aluminum with a walnut handle, a two-part design representing the transition from crude beans to refined coffee.

NOMAD SAUNA
Røssvatnet Lake, Varntresk, Norway
ARCHITECT: **Marco Casagrande and Hans-Petter Bjørnådal**

Marco Casagrande's Nomad City was a two-week workshop held on top of a frozen lake in the mountains of Norway. The Finnish architect brought together an interdisciplinary group of environmentalists, architects, and sociologists from Lund University to build a mobile city for nomads in response to nature. Creating a fishing shelter, a movable sauna, and an aurora observatory complete with fireplace for cooking, the team overcame harsh weather conditions to construct these intimate gathering places in the midst of the Norwegian wilderness.

SUMMERHOUSE INSIDE OUT HVALER

Papper, Hvaler Islands, Norway
ARCHITECT: **Reiulf Ramstad Arkitekter**

Reiulf Ramstad Arkitekter approach design with a strong conceptual vision. For example, their Summer Retreat Fuglevik near the coast in Moss, Norway, is designed according to the concept of a "mono-view," meaning that the house opens up to the landscape in one direction. Such a decisive design gives the indoor experience an unambiguous orientation and brings the landscape into the home.

For Summerhouse Inside Out Hvaler on the small island of Papper, the architects situated the home in the midst of an uncultivated landscape, interacting closely with its environs. Glass façades and windows allow nature to enter the house from every angle, and as the wooden exterior turns gray with age it will become one with the island.

VILLA HVEDEBJERGVEJ
Aarhus, Denmark
INTERIOR DESIGNER: **Sofie Ladefoged**, PHOTOGRAPHER: **Alex Tran**

Villa Hvedebjergvej is a brick house with rough walls, split levels, and large panoramic windows. Originally designed by architect Mogens Harborough in 1966, the home's original expressiveness has been maintained with its redecoration by Danish architect and interior designer Sofie Ladefoged. With rooms of yellow brick, black wood paneling, and beautiful hardwood floors, robust material choices for the decor combine classic modernist furniture with contemporary art and design, faithful to the house's cozy 1960s style. Today the house is just as durable, functional, and stylish as it was the day it was built.

VILLA
HVEDEBJERGVEJ

FERM LIVING

FERM LIVING
Copenhagen, Denmark

From baskets to bathrobes and cushions to cups, ferm LIVING delivers home products with retro charm and a graphic edge. Rooted in Danish design history, the wide array of ferm LIVING's products includes wallpaper and textiles, plus a large collection for kids. Materials include organic cotton, recycled paper, wool, wood, porcelain, and metal — favoring traditional materials manipulated by skilled craftsmen. Incorporating the recurring motifs of the house and the bird, these products are both homey and imaginative. In founder Trine Andersen's own words, "I have never created anything on the basis of strategy or cool calculation; it has to come from the heart."

SOKERI FABRIC

Helsinki, Finland
DESIGNER: **Hanna Konola**,
PRODUCER: **Kauniste**

Kauniste: inspirational everyday textiles. Combining the best of fresh design and traditional screenprinting skills, Kauniste prints original designs in water-based, solvent-free inks on linen-mix fabric. Linen is durable, absorbs moisture well, and dries quickly, making these textiles adaptable for a variety of uses. The company produces bags, tea towels, cushion covers, and aprons, among other things, and of course the fabric itself in available patterns, such as the Sokeri pattern designed by Finnish designer Hanna Konola. The pattern's shapes resemble sugar lumps — perhaps the reason the design is named Sokeri, which means "sugar."

OYOY LIVING DESIGN

Kibæk, Denmark
DESIGNER: **Lotte Fynboe**

The name OYOY is inspired by the letters OY, which since 1929 have adorned every Danish airplane. For OYOY Living Design, these characters symbolize its connection and commitment to Danish history. Primary designer Lotte Fynboe leads the company in creating functional high products from high-quality materials, such as the beech wood Tippetop candleholders, Japanese cushions, and a wide array of furniture for offices, kids' rooms, bedrooms, and communal living spaces. The young company sticks to Scandinavian elegance with undertones of Japanese style — always under the guidance of primary designer Fynboe's motto, modeled after Mies van der Rohe's famous saying, "less is more."

NORRGAVEL
DESIGNER: **Nirvan Richter**
Trångåsen, Jämtland, Sweden

According to designer Nirvan Richter, Norrgavel classic furniture often works best in an environment that contrasts with its highly contemporary design. Straightforward and original, the Norrgavel brand is distinguished by its harmonious, holistic design approach and the way its products integrate seamlessly into all types of homes. With traditional materials like soap-treated oak (a classic Danish finishing), Norrgavel designers are inspired by both the country and the city — bringing either a touch of the urban or a touch of nature to the opposing environment.

SUMMERHOUSE of ULRICA and DAVID BOGH-LIND

Gotland, Sweden

PHOTOGRAPHER: **Amelia Widell and Andreas Lönngren**

Situated on Gotland, Sweden's largest island in the Baltic Sea, Ulrica and David Bogh-Lind's breezy summer home is characterized by its fusion of Swedish style with influences from as far away as Morocco. The house's close interaction with surrounding nature adds to its romantic feel, clothed in thin white curtains and decorated with exotic prints, florals, and plaids. Walls and floors are variously treated throughout the home — from light, dark, and painted woods to white tiles. Basics from IKEA are intermingled with one-of-a-kind vintage finds and design classics to foster an eclectic, family-oriented home environment.

SUNDAY LAMP

Oslo, Norway
DESIGNER: **Frost Produkt together with Martina Carpelan**

Together with Martina Carpelan, Frost designed the Sunday Lamp. This lighting concept combines an (interchangeable) light source and shelf that can be mounted easily on any wall. Frost Produkt was established in Oslo in 2002, and its team currently includes five product and industrial designers from Norway and abroad.

Hans J Wegner

YOU+ME DYNAMO LAMP

Bergen, Norway
DESIGNER: **Siren Elise Wilhelmsen, Elisabeth Florstedt**,
PRODUCER: **Prototype**

You+Me is the product of teamwork between the object and its user: the user charges the lamp by pulling its cord, and the lamp's dynamo technology harnesses this energy to provide light. One minute of charging delivers 30 minutes of light free from power sources. Whether resting on a table, dangling from a hook, leaning on a branch, or hanging on the lamp's own supplementary rack system, the dynamo lamp is an energy-neutral item with a fresh design.

AFTEROOM CHAIR No.01

Stockholm, Sweden
DESIGNER: **Hung-Ming Chen**, PRODUCER: **Afteroom**

Big fans of Bauhaus, Afteroom designers created a chair that did away with unnecessary embellishment and reduced material usage to a bare minimum. The result was a minimalist style chair with a simple three-legged support connected to a backrest by a bent steel bar. In order to ensure the strength of the construction, the support system of Afteroom's chair is made of carefully welded solid steel bars — extremely firm and stable.

FISHERMAN'S COTTAGE
Gotland, Sweden
DESIGNER: **Bengan Widell**, PHOTOGRAPHER: **Karin Björkquist**

Whether designing furniture, clearing up a garden, or building a new house, Bengan Widell is a true jack-of-all-trades. In 1980, while canoeing in the waters of the Baltic Sea, Widell spotted a fisherman's cottage that he dreamed of renovating. In 2005 he was finally able to buy the land on which the cottage stands and has since made it into a special place on the cape. Surrounded by views of the sea and nestled into the surrounding trees, the home is a thoughtful, handmade, cozy update on a traditional cottage.

BIRD THROW
Finland
DESIGNER: **Klaus Haapaniemi and Mia Wallenius**

SPIDER WOOL SCARF
Finland
DESIGNER: **Klaus Haapaniemi and Mia Wallenius**

Klaus Haapeniemi design studio is influenced by nature, Finnish folklore, fantasy, and traditional
decorative arts — always with a contemporary twist. Artist Klaus Haapaniemi and designer Mia
Wallenius founded the design studio together in 2010, and though focusing on their luxurious textile collection they also work with furniture, fashion, books, and event and exhibition planning. They
enjoy collaborating with other designers to create limited edition pieces, though it could be said
that all of their projects have a one-of-a-kind feel. Using high-quality, functional materials, pieces
like their woven wool-silk mix Bird throw blanket and Spider wool scarf can work in any space,
whether rustic or modern.

.IU COPPER LAMP

Sweden

DESIGNER: **Daniella Witte with Fredrik Jönsson**

Stylist Daniella Witte's popular home blog has fresh ideas straight
from her home year-round. Attracted to dark tones, metals, and
greenery, Witte's style is geometric yet soft. Her .IU copper lamp
designs, made in collaboration with Fredrik Jönsson in 2012, lend
a sense of structure to a room with rustic copper piping and an
oversized bulb.

VILLA ASSERBO

Asserbo, Denmark

ARCHITECT: **Eentileen**, PHOTOGRAPHER: **Karsten Damstedt**

A woodland 60 kilometers north of Copenhagen is the site where Danish architecture firm Eentileen chose to construct its first digitally fabricated, sustainable, low-cost home. Teaming up with the fabricators at Facit Homes, the architects built Villa Asserbo using 820 sheets of plywood from sustainable Finnish timber. The house's digital design was fed into a CNC printer the size of a room, enabling them to shape the materials and construct the building in only four weeks. Most of the home's furnishings were produced in the same workshop as the architecture was, and its interior was styled by Hanne Vind to merge beautifully with the building's lines and the wooded surroundings.

clockwise:

₁ MEGA BULB SR₂
Copenhagen, Denmark
DESIGNER: **Sofie Refer**, PRODUCER: **&tradition**

₂ BLASTED
Copenhagen, Denmark
DESIGNER: **Kai Linke**, PRODUCER: **&tradition**

₃ BELLEVUE AJ₂ &
RAFT LOWSTOOL
Copenhagen, Denmark
DESIGNER: **Arne Jacobsen and Norm Architects**,
PRODUCER: **&tradition**

&TRADITION
Copenhagen, Denmark

Among the best-loved objects made by Danish design
company &tradition is the 45-degree cut Bellevue lamp,
originally designed in 1929 according to the Bauhaus style.
The new generation at &tradition picks up on the sleek
elegance of such timeless pieces to create new ideas like
the 2006 Mega Bulb SR2, designed by Sofie Refer, and the
2011 Blasted Lamp, designed by Kai Linke — new ideas for
today that may become the classics for the future.

HOUSE DOCTOR
Copenhagen, Denmark

It's clear from the titles of their collections that House Doctor is thoroughly Scandinavian, inspired by the duality of the Nordic seasons. In the Danish design firm's Autumn/Winter 2012 collection, themed "Nordic Lux," precious woods are used in harmony with a variety of metals, such as gold, silver, and copper. Such a stark contrast in material choices, reminiscent of a harsh Copenhagen winter, is the epitome of sharp, graphic, clean design. Yet the company's previous Spring/Summer collection — "Soft Summer" — reflects the other side of nature in the north: calm, warm, and beautiful. Employing natural materials like leather, wood, concrete, and raw iron, the colors of "Soft Summer" are lush, vivid, and expressive.

NEW NORM
Copenhagen, Denmark
INTERIOR DESIGNER: **Norm Architects**

New Norm is a dinnerware collection designed by Norm Architects that captures the special light of Scandinavia, taking materials, contours, and textures directly from natural elements with the simplicity and honesty that characterizes Nordic form. When designing the interior for the new Copenhangen restaurant Höst, Norm carried the philosophy of their product design to build a cozy, organic environment in an urban setting. In collaboration with Danish design house Menu, Norm chose to focus on materials that age gracefully — recycled wood, granite, old cast iron, and a dented sink — a offset by warm light and soft textiles.

HÖST
Copenhagen, Denmark
INTERIOR DESIGNER: **Norm Architects**

CONCRETE 02 PENDEL

Denmark
DESIGNER: **Bolia Design Team**, PRODUCER: **Bolia**

Bolia's dinnerware has attitude — items like a coarse concrete lamp that comes in three different shapes and sizes are bold yet understated. This and other Bolia home products are manufactured once they are ordered — each piece is made by hand from scratch.

HOME of NETTA-NATALIA

Vaasa, Finland

DESIGNER: **Netta-Natalia Löytynoja**

Incorporating elegant, well-known design objects with vintage, found, and homemade materials, Finnish designer and photographer Netta-Natalia is a master at interior decoration. Living in an old factory building that she has updated and adorned herself, she favors a muted palette of black, white, and gray when it comes to textiles and furniture. In her industrial-style dining space, for example, a sturdy black lamp by 360volt hangs over a homemade steel-gray table and black and white chairs by Eames and Ilmari Tapiovaara — adorned with fresh-flowers in a simple glass jar.

BEOPLAY A9
Struer, Denmark
DESIGNER: **Øivind Alexander Slaatto**, PRODUCER: **Bang & Olufsen**

Bang & Olufsen never ceases to amaze — the company's innovative audio and visual innovations always combine unique design with the latest technology. With the BeoPlay A9 speaker system, the typical bulky sound-transmitting device has been transformed into a sleek, spherical piece of furniture. The A9 has no strings attached: completely wireless, the volume of the speaker is controlled by simply swiping a hand across its rounded top edge. This functional show-stopper, like all of the company's products, is inspired by classic Danish minimalist furniture design — and available in many colors.

RUSTIC AND NEW IN SKÅNE

Skåne, Sweden

ARCHITECT: **Tommy Carlson**, PHOTOGRAPHER: **Jonas Ingerstedt**

Completed over the course of three years by Swedish architect Tommy Carlson, this Skåne apartment became a live workshop for evolving architecture within its building. This project was completed over three-year period, and during that time its design changed course according to the way it was lived in — built-in seating and even hammocks were added for perfect ease and comfort. The home's gorgeous open space retained much of the building's original structure, while other original details were refined, like the dark exposed ceiling beams, and many new features were invented — like a spectacular enclosed staircase hovering above the floor.

EMMA OLBERS
Gothenburg, Sweden

Emma Olbers grew up on a farm outside of Gothenburg, Sweden. Upon moving to Stockholm to begin craft training, she fell in love with design, and after working for various companies, including IKEA, she opened her own studio in 1999. Her work incorporates her personal history and connection to the land; she retains an environmental awareness through material selection and thoughtful participation in the production process. One example of such investment was her Stockholm Wood exhibition shown at Designgalleriet during the Stockholm Furniture Fair 2012. Olbers wanted to make furniture from raw material found in downtown Stockholm — and then to figure out whether consumers felt more personally attached to furniture if they knew which tree the wood came from.

MINGUS PENDANTS

Copenhagen, Denmark
DESIGNER: **Cecilie Manz**, PRODUCER: **Lightyears**

The Mingus Pendant lamps designed by Cecilie Manz and produced by Danish company Lighyears have become known for their distinctive and dramatic figures. A balance of masculine construction and feminine lines, the plunging pendant lends drama to any room and the depth of the elegant laquered lampshade prevents glare.

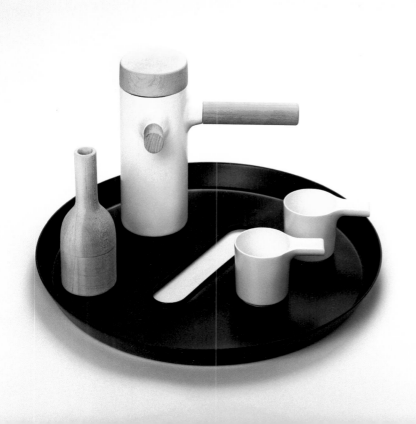

TIMES

Norway
DESIGNER: **Fredrik Wærnes**, PRODUCER: **Strek Collective**

Times is a collection of tableware consisting of a coffee pot, milk carafe, sugar shaker, and cups. The shapes of the objects are inspired by traditional equipment for outdoor brewing of coffee and, with a simplified design, symbolize the cultural separation of times between now and then.

ALL SO BRIGHT

A bunk bed built of OSB board is the main piece of furniture in the playful room shared by two children. The lower part of the wall is painted a bright green with a scalloped edge to the white upper part, which is covered by framed children's drawings and crafts. Above the pink vintage sofa, filled with patterned cushions, sits a shallow shelf adorned with colorful children's books and a couple of art prints with circus motifs. Toys are stored in kitchen cabinets placed in a long row along one of the walls; with a plywood board placed on top they double as a work and play table. The strong colors seem to have overflowed into the rest of the apartment in the form of modern art that fills every room and brightly painted furniture and accessories that really stand out against the white walls. Some unexpected features are the neon yellow kitchen ceiling, the big taxidermy swan sitting on the livingroom floor and the big collection of colorful sneakers that is displayed by the entrance.

What defines this style is the playful use of colors and materials and the eccentric details that add a very personal touch. A brave use of neon or primary colors can be seen on anything from floors or ceilings to small details like vases or lamps. Untraditional materials such as OSB or plywood are used in new ways, creating a very contemporary feeling. Thought-provoking art in the form of modern photography, abstract paintings, or cartoon-style art prints is mixed with children's drawings and DIY pieces. Inspiration is drawn from anything from 1980's discos to Alice in Wonderland to create an adventurous, fresh, and playful atmosphere where creativity and invention is highly celebrated.

HUMLEGÅRDEN APARTMENT
Engelbrektsgatan, Stockholm, Sweden
ARCHITECT: **Tham & Videgård Arkitekter**, PHOTOGRAPHER: **Åke E:son Lindman**

The Humlegården apartment by Swedish Tham & Videgård Arkitekter relates directly to its Stockholm setting near Humlegården Park, where the greenery changes with the seasons. The designers pushed the limits of the traditional Swedish use of color and pattern, bridging cultural history with the apartment's natural context. The overlapping colors of the parquet floor made from ash wood hit the right note between old and new, and link the various spaces throughout the floor plan. Conversing with the original architecture of this turn-of-the-century art nouveau flat, each piece of parquet coating the floor and climbing the walls was selected to create continuity, yet remain complex enough to form the backdrop for a variety of furniture and decor.

FRITZ HANSEN

Allerød, Denmark

PHOTOGRAPHER: Ditte Isager

Behind the world-famous Fritz Hansen brand is the story of a
family of Danish cabinetmakers who revolutionized Scandinavian
design, producing some of the world's most revered design classics. The Fritz Hansen company has developed a corporate culture
characterized by the love of good craftsmanship and a desire to
make the most of modern industrial production methods. From the
iconic Arne Jacobsen's Egg and Swan chairs, first designed in 1958,
to Jaime Hayon's Jacobsen-inspired Favn sofa, launched in 2011,
Fritz Hansen has continued its tradition of creative partnerships
with visionary designers and architects over the last 135 years.

TULIP CHAIR and WOMB SOFA
Finland
DESIGNER: **Eero Saarinen**, PRODUCER: **Knoll**,
PHOTOGRAPHER: **Joshua McHugh**

Eero Saarinen was not afraid of bold shapes and colors. Though lauded as a pioneer of sleek and minimal design, the Finnish designer's chairs, such as the iconic Tulip chair and Womb sofa-chair, are distinctive enough to be recognized in any living room today. Not only noticeable and iconic, Saarinen's work is still perfectly functional and modern five decades after his passing.

SAARINEN SIDE CHAIR
and COFFEE TABLE
Finland
DESIGNER: **Eero Saarinen,** PRODUCER: **Knoll**
PHOTOGRAPHER: **Joshua McHugh** (left),
Richard Power (right)

FLAG HALYARD CHAIR

Allerød, Denmark

DESIGNER: **Hans J. Wegner**, PRODUCER: **PP Møbler**

Danish design icon Hans J. Wegner trained as a cabinet-maker before attending the Copenhagen School of Arts and Crafts. Working for Arne Jacobsen and Erik Moller's architecture practice, he set up his own office in 1943. Throughout his life until his death in 2007 he designed furniture exclusively for Johannes and Fritz Hansen; today, Fritz Hansen still proudly manufactures and markets Wegner's pieces. From the modest, pleasant Peacock chair to the endearing, inviting Teddy Bear chair to the sophisticated, angular Flag Halyard chair, the lasting popularity of Wegner's work suggests that good design can stand the test of time.

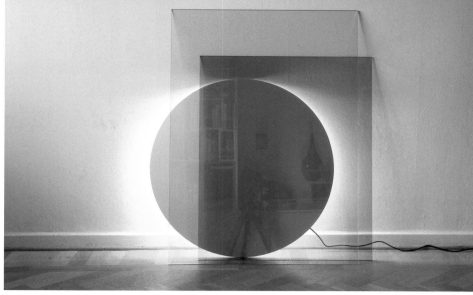

LIGHT TRAY and COLOUR
Oslo, Norway
DESIGNER: **Daniel Rybakken & Andreas Engesvik Studio,** PRODUCER: **Spazio Rossana Orlandi and Ligne Roset**

Daniel Rybakken's Light Tray is an artificial plane that obscures its power source and creates the illusion of self-powered illumination, with tinted hand-blown glass domes that can be reconfigured. His Colour lighting concept is the result of a collaboration with Andreas Engesvik. Produced by Ligne Roset, Colour is a freestanding adjustable lamp that allows the creation of light compositions using various colored diffusors.

HALO
Copenhagen, Denmark
DESIGNER: **Nina Bruun**

It may seem counterintuitive to take inspiration from a total solar eclipse when designing a lamp, but Nina Bruun's Halo lamp expertly adopts the concept of indirect light to provide a unique atmosphere. Low-temperature LED bulbs, which can sometimes provide sterile-seeming light, are employed in this case in a warm, inviting way behind a copper disk.

ANDREAS ENGESVIK
Product Designer | Oslo, Norway

TRADITION MEETS INNOVATION IN TIMELESS DESIGN

The strong unity between function and form reflected in the works of Andreas Engesvik may be most easily described as Scandinavian. Yet his use of diverse materials — such as cast iron, cork, glass, wood, and wool — lends them an emotionality that is clearly unique.

After receiving a bachelor's degree in art history from the University of Bergen, Engesvik went on to acquire a master's in design at the National College of Art and Design in 2000. In the same year, together with designers Torbjørn Anderssen and Espen Voll, he cofounded the design collective Norway Says, which received accolades for its products and drew international attention to the Norwegian design scene.

Engesvik opened his own studio in 2009, and has created diverse objects that move between industrial design and arts and crafts, including furniture, accessories, sculpture, and even a bicycle. His Norwegian and international clients include littala, Muuto, Ligne Roset, and Asplund.
 2007 Engesvik received the Torsten and Wanja Söderberg Prize, the 2009 Wallpaper* Design Award, and the 2010 iF Product Design award. He is also a professor at the University College of Arts, Crafts and Design (Konstfack) in Stockholm.

The products you have designed are, in the very best sense of the word, quintessentially Scandinavian. Would you describe them like that as well? If so, what is that Scandinavian element in your work?

The Scandinavian element in my work is probably my approach to what products should be with regard to their functionality and appearance. Scandinavian designers are quite practical, and there is a strong emphasis on understanding the product, on the selection of materials, and on how things are manufactured.
 I think that we learn a lot about functionality growing up in Scandinavia through typical activities like sailing, skiing, staying in a winter cabin, and so on. My son is eight years old — and he already has his own axe.

Scandinavian design is represented by a number of old masters but also an impressive amount of successful contemporary designers and brands.

Do you have a favorite item designed by one of the old masters?

I think there is an important continuity in the Scandinavian tradition that still has relevance. The old masters have always inspired many designers, and I think the new simplicity that evolved in the 1990s revitalized the Scandinavian tradition in a very positive way.
 I don't have a particular favorite work by an old master at the moment — there are so many to choose from in the period from 1960 to 1970.

What is your impression of the current Nordic design scene? What about the differences or similarities in the design work emerging from the various Scandinavian countries?

While there are coherent traits in the Scandinavian approach towards form and working with

aspects of functionality, it is difficult to point out particular differences between the Scandinavian countries. It is important to remember that many Scandinavian designers work internationally — and that this affects how products turn out.

Your Bunad blankets, developed in cooperation with the Norwegian textile company Mandal Veveri, were inspired by various regional patterns found in traditional Norwegian folk costumes (*bunad*). Are there any other particular historic or cultural elements that inspire you in your work?

I am not so interested in the terms "new" and "old" as separate entities, although my degree in art history might influence my aesthetic choices. One of the courses I teach as a guest professor at Konstfack in Stockholm has the title "New — Old — New." The course was about how we interpret objects and how they are all constructed from layers of meaning. We are surrounded by things old and new — and they are all carriers of meaning.

Your projects show a dedication to material. How do you approach the materials with which you work?

I think it is natural to work with materials that are familiar to you. At the moment I am fascinated by glass, ceramics, wool, and solid wood. Colors are also important to me, but they are often added in the last phase of a project.

"At the moment I am fascinated by glass, ceramics, wool, and solid wood. Colors are also important to me, but they are often added in the last phase of a project."

What was the idea behind your design collective Norway Says?

When I founded Norway Says, it was about finding new arenas for my products. At the time, the market for design was nonexistent in Norway.

The most important thing Norway Says achieved was that we left a footprint showing young Norwegian designers and students that there is always a market for good products. Still, as a designer in Norway one must work internationally.

For some of your lighting projects you collaborated with Norwegian designer Daniel Rybakken. Could you describe that project and collaboration?

The collaboration with Daniel Rybakken has been great — he is a good friend and colleague. We first started working together in 2005/2006, when he did a internship at my old studio. Rybakken has a very precise approach to ideas and form. He is what I describe as a complete designer. His position and success is a big inspiration for the Norwegian design field.

I also collaborate with the Norwegian studio StokkeAustad — they are also really talented. Running my own studio allows me to collaborate with various colleagues in a free and inspiring way.

You are also teaching design. What are your students learning from you?

In general, I think students must learn how to become independent in their ideas, approach, and mindset. And also how teamwork can also create space for creative development.

I also think it's important to be a responsible designer. With this I mean striving to make design that lasts. Product design at its best is about making good and relevant products in a conscious way, in terms of production, quality, and so on — this also depends a lot on the manufacturer.

Finally, the global design market today is interesting and in a moment of change that offers great opportunities. To quote George Nelson, "There is always a market for good design."

WORLDFLEX HOME
Frederiksværk, Denmark
ARCHITECT: **Arcagency**, INTERIOR ARCHITECT: **Tina Midtgaard**

The WorldFLEX housing concept is a patented modular building
system based on 40-foot-high standard modules. The structure
can be adapted to personal needs, as well as local climate or
geographic challenges, and is the first pre-fabricated housing
system that meets the demands of the international environmental building standard. A completed home, implemented in
Frederiksværk, Denmark by the architects at Arcagency, was
made beautiful by the interior architect Tina Midtgaard. The
180-square-meter home's interior design conveys the same
values as the house itself — all furniture is made from environmentally friendly materials and retains the essence of Danish
furniture design.

THE APARTMENT

Copenhagen, Denmark

INTERIOR DESIGNER: **Tina Seidenfaden Busck and Pernille Hornhaver**, PHOTOGRAPHER: **Alastair Halfide**

The Apartment's showroom creates a new universe of design objects, furniture, antiques, and art. Innovative modern design meets the unparalleled craft of traditional furniture making. Founders Tina Seidenfaden Busck and Pernille Hornhaver edit interior design pieces with an international point of view, exhibiting world-renowned designers such as Michael Anastassiades and McCollin Bryan along handpicked vintage pieces.

THE APARTMENT

TINA SEIDENFADEN BUSCK

Interior Designer, THE APARTMENT | Copenhagen, Denmark

AT HOME WITH DYNAMIC VISIONS OF DESIGN AND ART

The Apartment is a showroom of a different kind. Instead of a sterile gallery where items are presented out of context, here design objects, furniture, antiques, and art are arranged as they could be in the comfort of one's own home.

Situated in the heart of Copenhagen, The Apartment is the brainchild of Tina Seidenfaden Busck and Pernille Hornhaver. The two decided to set up shop in a handsomely restored eighteenth-century apartment.

Since 2010, The Apartment has offered a rotating exhibition of items curated from an international point of view, serving as a shop as much as an inspiring showcase of the interior design and art purchasing consultation services the two also offer. The founders have a tight network with international galleries and auction houses, allowing The Apartment to showcase and sell works by renowned international artists.

You are located in Copenhagen. What is special about Copenhagen that makes it so good for design?

Copenhagen and Denmark in general have a long design tradition and a very professional design industry. Design is considered one of our strongest areas of competence and thus receives a lot of political and economic attention. I think that helps to create a fertile environment for our designers.

Please explain the concept behind The Apartment and how this came about.

The idea behind The Apartment was to create a space where we could place vintage furniture and contemporary art and design in more inspiring and homey settings than the traditional gallery space offers.

We wanted to offer an alternative vision of a modern home that could both inspire and surprise. It all came together when we found the perfect location, a 200-square-meter apartment in an eighteenth-century building in need of extensive renovation. It has been a labor of love to implement all the details we would like to see in our own homes.

From your perspective and experience what are the key ingredients to a good atmosphere in a private space?

A certain boldness of spirit and an easygoing atmosphere. Try not to focus too much on matching colors and styles; a vintage design from the 1950s can take on a whole new meaning in a contemporary setting and vice versa. We like to mix iconic furniture designs from the 1950s with contemporary art and design, adding cozy and less formal elements like Moroccan vintage rugs and antique textiles.

First and foremost, we look for items that bear the mark of true craftsmanship and that add personality and character to your home.

What defines Scandinavian design for you?

Traditionally, Scandinavian design has been synonymous with the functional and minimalist style of Danish Modern. In The Apartment, we like to combine that style with the more colorful and ornamented Swedish furniture designs from that same period. We are very much inspired by Josef Frank's work for Svenskt Tenn, the design company that really established Swedish Modern design in the 1950s.

Looking for Scandinavian spaces one comes across a lot of very light, white, beige, and/or gray spaces. The Apartment also uses color in a friendly, even playful manner. Please describe your use of color and light.

Colors add life and character to a home, whether they come from your furniture, a full bookshelf, rugs, or artwork. I use colors and light to establish both elegance and coziness in a home.

At The Apartment you exhibit not only Scandinavian designers and artists. What would you consider as the Scandinavian element in your work/your approach?

We live in a country where the long winter only leaves eight to nine hours of daylight, thus we have a strong focus on lighting. We are lucky to have partnered up with Michael Anastassiades, who makes exquisite handmade designs fabricated in small family-run workshops. His lighting designs have a strong sculptural element with beautiful finishings in materials like marble and polished brass.

Another Scandinavian aspect is our predilection for wooden furniture; we work with Københavns Møbelsnedkeri (Copenhagen furniture carpentry), which has designed our

"We live in a country where the long winter only leaves eight to nine hours of daylight, thus we have a strong focus on lighting."

THIS PAGE (CLOCKWISE):

1: Tina Seidenfaden Busck's appreciation for fine craftsmanship and keen sense of style is apparent in her own apartment's bold mix of iconic design furniture, contemporary art, and vintage elements, including a Josef Frank daybed, an Eames sofa table, a side table by Mc-Collin Bryan, artwork by Olafur Eliasson and Gert and Uwe Tobias, plus a vintage Beni Ouarain tribal rug, and a floral armchair picked up at a flea market.

2: Busk is also selling a rare edition of the Flagline Chair by Hans J. Wegner, c. 1950, Tinted Lens Table by McCollin Bryan, 2012, Michael Anastassiades Ball Light, 2008, accompanied by a vintage Murano vase and vintage Moroccan rag rug.

3: A well-curated mix of old and new: Easy Chair upholstered with sheepskin with stained beech armrests and legs, designed by Martin Olsen, ca. 1952. Onyx Light by Michael Anastassiades, 2007, a French folding screen from the 1950s, and artwork by Copenhagen-based, Israeli artist Tal R.

modern and very elegant dining tables and wardrobe solutions in smoked oak and glass.

What is your perspective on the great masters of Scandinavian design vs. the current generation?

Danish Modern has been both a blessing and a curse for the new generation of designers. The golden age we experienced in the 1950s established Danish design worldwide, but this position, of course, has been challenged since the late 1960s. The Danish contemporary designers that we work with master the balance between the functionalist heritage and a more contemporary touch.

However, we don't have a particular focus on Danish design as such; we travel a lot and like to discover new international designers that haven't yet made it to the Northern European market.

LOKAL
Helsinki, Finland
PHOTOGRAPHER: **Katja Hagelstam**

Lokal is a concept gallery in Helsinki run by Katja Hagelstam. Hagelstam, also a freelance photographer specializing in antiques, interiors, and food, selects and showcases top Finnish contemporary art, craft, and design in Lokal's relaxed setting. Along with a steady selection of new and vintage objects from coffee cups to handicrafts, every second month, an exhibition featuring the work of an up-and-coming designer goes up at Lokal. A gallery and a store, Lokal is also a cafe, offering coffee to drink inside or take away.

HOME of JESSICA FOLCKER and DANIEL HECKSCHER

Outside of Stockholm, Sweden
STYLIST: **Myrica Bergqvist**, PHOTOGRAPHER: **Carl Dahlstedt**

Swedish singer Jessica Folcker and her husband, interior architect Daniel Heckscher, purchased a house just outside Stockholm in need of an update — but it had several unique features that deserved care and preservation. Without changing the exterior façade or the interior atmosphere, the simple home originally designed by architect Tore Axen was modernized with fresh pops of color, new and vintage furniture, and works of art, accenting the original plan and complementing the beautiful window views of nature.

STUDIO of GAMFRATESI
Copenhagen, Denmark

Gam and Enrico Fratesi are a Danish-Italian team who founded the studio GamFratesi in 2006. The duo have a throroughly Scandinavian grounding with global touches and influences, expanding the realm of traditional Danish design. Based in Copenhagen, they travel for research and exhibitions all over the world, borrowing often from Italian aesthetics and minimalist Japanese concepts to seek creative fusions of function and form through unified solutions.

REWRITE
Copenhagen, Denmark
DESIGNER: **GamFratesi**, PRODUCER: **Lignet Roset**

A perfect example of GamFratesi's fusion of concept and design, the Rewrite desk provides an "isolated work bubble," carving out an intimate workspace from even the busiest office environment.

BULB FICTION
Copenhagen, Denmark
DESIGNER: **KiBiSi**, PRODUCER: **Lightyears**

KiBiSi design group is an idea-driven firm that has become influential in today's world of Scandinavian design — working across a range of disciplines, the team creates everything from furniture and household objects to bicycles and aircraft. The Bulb Fiction bulb is just one of their unique products: it is a classic lightbulb shape that has been scaled up and converted into a streamlined unit to be hung from the ceiling. The bulb, produced by Lightyears, is noticeable from its hand-blown, voluminous shape and white silicone-covered cord. The fixture creates the illusion of a classic incandescent bulb, hiding the low-energy light source within and ensuring soft, radiating light.

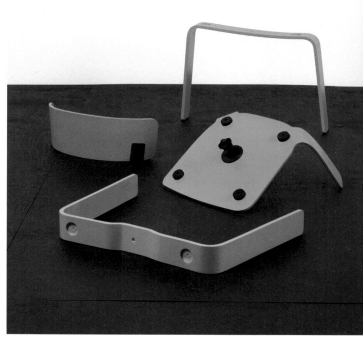

BENTO CHAIR
and PLUG LAMP

Stockholm, Sweden
DESIGNER: **Form Us With Love**,
PRODUCER: **One Nordic**

When Form Us With Love design studio created their first product, the team decided on
the most iconic possibility: the chair. Because
they planned to sell products online to international customers, the designers considered the
question of effective shipping first — and came
up with an inventive, do-it-yourself design. The
Bento chair arrives in pieces in a small box, easy
to assemble without sacrificing quality design.
This creative approach is representative of the
studio's overall attitude — whether invent-
ing lamps that plug directly into the wall (Plug
Lamp) or coming up with efficient and stylish
spatial solutions.

VERSO
Finland/Sweden
DESIGNER: **Mikko Halonen**, PRODUCER: **One Nordic**

Verso is a shelving system designed by Finnish designer Mikko Halonen for One Nordic. Available in black, white, and natural wood, the versatile ladder units can be used to hang anything from clothes to books to accessories. Manufactured in Sweden, the ladder breaks down into small pieces that can be easily assembled at home.

HOME of RIIKA KANTINKOSKI

Espoo, Finland
DESIGNER and PHOTOGRAPHER: **Riikka Kantinkoski**

Finnish photographer and designer Riikka Kantinkoski is inspired by simple, timeless design with an individual spirit. Her home is a blend of her own design pieces, like playful posters, kitchen items, and a homemade coat rack. She's even incorporated one of her designs as a wall painting in one room and customized every surface and project down to a hanging plant holder made from cardboard and macrame yarn.

MIRROR HOUSE

Copenhagen, Denmark

ARCHITECT: **MLRP**

Danish-American architects MLRP transformed an existing graffiti-covered playground structure in Copenhagen's newly renovated Central Park into an inviting reflective pavilion as part of the city's new Interactive Playground Project. Fun-house mirrors were mounted on the gabled ends and behind the doors of the structure, reflecting the surrounding park and its activity. At night, the mirrored shutters are closed, but during the day the whole building opens up, attracting children to come see themselves reflected in the polished stainless steel. The interior layout of the pavilion was modified slightly and upgraded regarding insulation and functional design.

YOUTH CENTER in JYLLINGE

Roskilde, Denmark

ARCHITECT: **Cornelius + Vöge**, PHOTOGRAPHER: **Adam Mørk**

Cornelius + Vöge's conversion and extension of an existing building in the Danish village of Jyllinge is a re-interpretation of the red barns and fisherman's cabins in the old part of the village, bridging the older area with a newer 1970s development nearby. Used as a recreation center for Jyllinge's youth, the building contains a multipurpose concert hall, indoor and outdoor sports arenas, and an integrated climbing wall. Borrowing the region's traditional red color to preserve the town's identity, the youth center is now low-energy, playful, and functional for the youth of today.

HOME of ERIK and CATHY WESTRELL NORDSTRÖM

Vasastan, Stockholm, Sweden
DESIGNER: **Erik and Cathy Westrell Nordström**, PHOTOGRAPHER:
Patric Johansson

When graphic designer Cathy Westrell Nordström and her husband
Erik Nordström redesigned their own late nineteenth-century
apartment in Vasastan, Stockholm, they decided to stick to a white
palette — beyond that, they didn't have any rules. Primarily following her minimal Scandinavian taste, Cathy also looked to American
designers for inspiration in combining layers and colors. Selecting
a mix of furniture from mid-century Danish designers like Borge
Mogensen and Arne Jacobsen, and new pieces like a Howard sofa,
the duo scoured both flea markets and design shops like Asplund
in Stockholm, where they found their dining table. Enamored by
the home's high ceilings and beautiful molding, they left plenty of
space for the architecture to breathe but infused the apartment
fully with their own style.

BIRKEGADE ROOFTOP PENTHOUSES
Copenhagen, Denmark
ARCHITECT: **JDS / Julien De Smedt Architects**

The Elmegarde district is one of the most densely populated areas of inner Nørrebro in Copenhagen. Responding to the district's cramped courtyards, JDS Architects decided to replace the "missing garden" of this apartment on the roof of an existing housing block which had been recently topped with a new penthouse. The rooftop playground with a green-hill grass garden has a shock-absorbing surface, playful suspension bridge, outdoor kitchen and barbeque, wooden deck, and dramatic raised viewing platform. Optimizing the possibilities for a rooftop space, the residents are not only provided with additional living space and play area but a beautiful view of the surrounding city.

HOUSING PROJECT UGLEVEIEN

Oslo, Norway
ARCHITECT: **Espen Surnevik**, PHOTOGRAPHER: **Ragnar Hartvig**

With over ten years of experience, Espen Surnevik Architects develop unique functional solutions for customized spaces and specific clients. Ranging from cottages to villas to nurseries and university buildings, principal designer Espen Surnevik's projects, such as the housing project Ugleveien in Oslo, are practical, stylish, and bright. For Ugleveien, Surnevik converted a neoclassical architectural space into a modern family home, safeguarding the feeling of being in an old house but incorporating modern amenities like tucked-away storage units and a fantastic contemporary children's room.

DEAR DISASTER

Malmö, Sweden

DESIGNER: **Jenny Ekdahl**

Inspired by fascinating yet terrifying natural forces, Jenny Ekdahl's Dear Disaster consists of a reversible wooden structure that encourages individual interaction and stimulates creativity. The conceptual piece is meant to facilitate a process of reconciliation with nature after a natural disaster by giving the user an outlet through which feelings can be expressed, aiding in the psychological recovery process. An array of 2,000 wooden scales marking the beech wood surface resembles water patterns but also images and graphs of natural disasters.

KENNO CHAIR

Helsinki, Finland
DESIGNER: **Järvi Ruoho**, PRODUCER: **Showroom Finland**

The Kenno chair is made from a new kind of recycled cardboard. The sturdy yet lightweight material can be recycled as paper; only water-based adhesives are used to solidify its sandwich construction. The lightweight material is durable and versatile, and its surface can even be drawn on. The ingenious chair is produced by Showroom Finland and was designed by Heikki Ruoho of the company Järvi Ruoho, a joint effort between him and fellow Finnish designer Teemu Järvi. The Helsinki-based company, whose name means "lake and grass," produces practical solutions spanning the broad fields of industrial, furniture, interior, and concept design.

CLARA VON ZWEIGBERGK

Product Designer | Stockholm, Sweden

SUBLIME WHIMSY THROUGH COLOR AND FORM

A certain lightheartedness pervades the work of Clara von Zweigbergk, but it is one that is sharpened by the precision of lines and meticulous attention to color combinations. Recent examples include her iconic, prism-like mobiles for Artecnica and Vitra and her polygonal tray system for Hay — the latter of which was recognized in 2012 by the Swedish National Design Award for being "simple and ingenious."

After studying graphic design and illustration in her native Stockholm and at the Art Center College of Design in Pasadena, California, von Zweigbergk worked with advertising agencies and designers in Los Angeles, Milan, and Stockholm. Cofounding Riveran Design Studio in Stockholm in 1997, she worked across disciplines, collaborating within the worlds of fashion, illustration, architecture, furniture, and product and graphic design. She then worked in Milan at Lissoni Associati as a senior graphic designer for clients such as Boffi, Armani, and Alessi.

Now back with an own studio in Stockholm since 2006, von Zweigbergk pursues her great interest in paper, color, typography, and handicraft through projects ranging from corporate identities, art direction, packaging, and book design, along with a growing series of products. She also teaches at her alma mater, Beckmans College of Design.

There is a playful use of color in your projects, which is a nice contrast to the subtle color palette often found in Scandinavian design. How would you describe the way you work with color?

You can express and communicate so much with colors, which have always played an important role in my work. I choose colors by intuition. Over the years I have matured in my approach towards color. This has made me more easygoing with regard to choices — I can find beauty in nearly all colors — but I can also be quite stubborn in getting them exact.

Do you see a certain Scandinavian element in your work? What is that element?

I am constantly peeling off the layers of my creations to achieve simplicity — even though I sometimes wish I could go crazy with fifteen fonts and images. But I just can't! That must be Sweden's doing.

There are a number of true masters of Scandinavian design. Do you have any favorites?

Of the many masters of Scandinavian design, Arne Jacobsen, is one of my favorites. But to be honest, I am much more a fan of Italian design and also of the Eames's work.

How would you describe the contemporary Scandinavian design scene? Are there trends you see as a professor of design in the youngest generation of designers?

There is a lot of interesting design being created by the younger generation. You also see less of a gap between art and design now than before. Also, I am happy to see that many of them are taking sustainability into consideration in the design process.

Sustainability — does this play a role in your work and approach as well?

When it is up to me, sustainability does play a role, even if on a small scale. For instance, with regard to the selection of paper and other materials. Also if objects are produced close by, this reduces the carbon footprint associated with long-distance shipping.

You worked in the United States and Italy before setting up your studio in your native Stockholm. What is different about the approach to design, the expectations of clients?

In Milan, design and fashion is central, and the design scene is big and international. This makes the clients more informed. For me, it was a pleasure to work with so many passionate designers as well as clients who have a good understanding and appreciation of design.

When I was in Los Angeles, I experienced a wonderful attitude of everything being possible. In the United States there seems to be more of a focus on the market than in Italy or Sweden, which places more demands on the design work to create something that is both well designed as well as commercially successful.

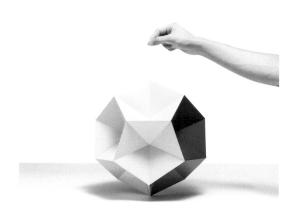

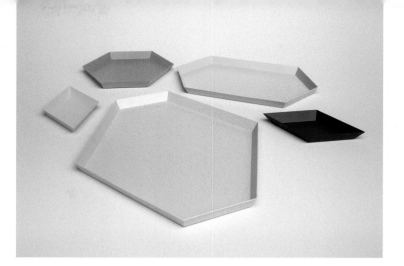

Commercial success — is this something you think your students should aim for as well?

I don't teach a commercial mindset. More importantly, I am hoping to inspire my students to work more by hand and to discover the freedom it gives. About 10 years ago, I discovered a great desire to return to working in a more analog way. I made a promise to myself to let the computer rest more often. Working only digitally you can only go as far as your computer skills take you. But with a pen, paper, and scissors you can come up with anything. Often it takes no time at all trying out a 3-D idea in paper, compared to doing a rendering.

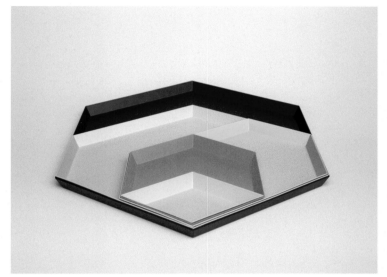

Your recent projects reflect geometric forms. What's next?

I am still exploring various aspects of the geometric typology, but for the last six months or so there have been a lot more dots, with black and white, as well as more muted colors, in my work than before. My ideas often occur to me intuitively, so I can't really say what will happen next!

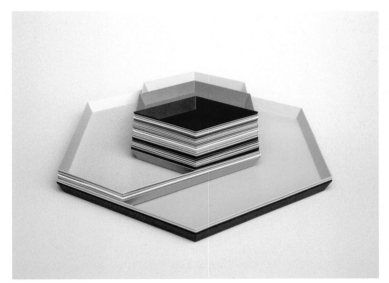

LEFT PAGE:

Themis Mobile Mono, a large, 12 in./30 cm dodecahedron, launched by Artecnica, 2012.

THIS PAGE (CLOCKWISE):

1 Themis Prism mobile with five paper ornaments, inspired by polyhedra, launched by Artecnica, 2012.
2 Kaleido tray series in powder-coated steel, launched by Hay, 2012.

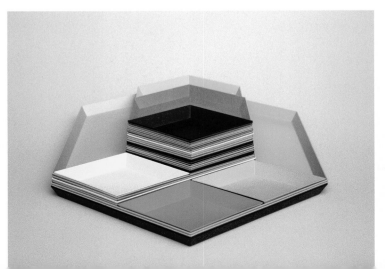

THE WOOD LAMP

Copenhagen, Denmark
DESIGNER: **TAF Architects**, PRODUCER: **Muuto**

The Finnish word *muutos* means "new perspective," and in Muuto's case, this perspective is friendly, colorful, and sometimes even romantic. Muuto works with a variety of prominent designers, who are given the freedom necessary to invent new ideas. TAF Architects designed the Wood Lamp for Muuto to be a low-tech antidote to the modern desk lamp. All the lamp's details are pragmatically chosen and every screw is visible.

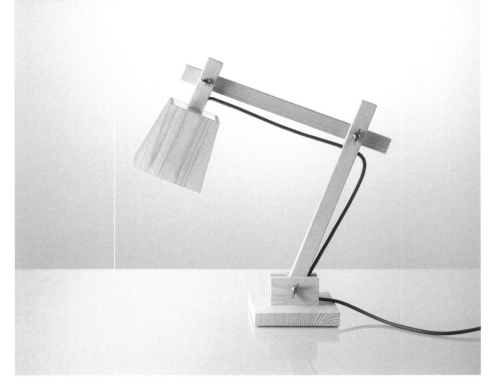

BAMBI TABLE

Oslo, Norway
DESIGNER: **Caroline Olsson**

Caroline Olsson's Bambi table can be used at two different levels, as either a coffee table or dining table. The table's leg joints resemble the knees of a deer, which can bend in one direction but remain upright and stable when locked. Olsson is a Norwegian designer whose products have been nominated for numerous awards for their lighthearted and innovative character.

GRADIENT SACKS

Helsinki, Finland

DESIGNER: **Susanna Vento**, PRODUCER: **Varpunen**

"We made the first sack for our daughter's bath toys, and suddenly many of our friends wanted them too." This is the simple story behind Susanna Vento and her husband Jussi's Varpunen Sack: a practical sack with infinite possibilities — indoor or outdoor, kitchen or bathroom, office or balcony. Susanna, an interior designer, and Jussi, who runs a print company, work together to design and construct the popular product in a variety of sizes and patterns. The Finnish duo released the first Varpunen Sack in 2011, and its possibilities continue to expand.

TINT
Oslo, Norway
DESIGNER: **Kristine Five Melvaer**

Norwegian designer Kristine Five Melvaer investigates the way objects communicate and create emotional bonds, bridging the disciplines of product design and graphic design. Translating emotional qualities into sensuous objects with a Scandinavian simplicity, Melvaer's work is often inspired by nature — like a series of room dividers called Tint, sheer printed sheets of silk fabric that move as people pass through a space. These dividers question spatial separation, being fragile and organic alternatives to rigid room separations.

GEO THERMOS
and BLOCK TABLE
Copenhagen, Denmark
DESIGNER: **Simon Legald and Nicholai Wiig Hansen,**
PRODUCER: **Normann Copenhagen**

Normann's Geo thermos is a minimalistic thermos design composed of unusually sharp geometric shapes fused with bright and lively color combinations. The thermoses, designed by Nicholai Wiig Hansen, are made from thermoplastic to keep hot coffee warm.

The Block table is a light and airy side table on wheels, designed by Simon Legald for Normann Copenhagen. As a side table, tea or coffee table, minibar, or bedside table, Block is mobile and versatile — not to mention streamlined. The item is carefully built from ash wood and steel and has been launched in mint green, light gray, and dark gray.

NERD CHAIR
Copenhagen, Denmark
DESIGNER: **David Geckeler,** PRODUCER: **Muuto**

David Geckeler's Nerd chair has a unique personality. Though the chair's innovative integration between its seat and back and precise detailing are contemporary ideas, its overall form, material, and craftsmanship reference classic Scandinavian design values.

THE TRUE HISTORY OF TEA

VICTOR H. MAIR & ERLING HOH

CHARIOT
Copenhagen, Denmark
DESIGNER: **GamFratesi**, PRODUCER: **Casamania**

GamFratesi's memorable Chariot side table is composed of two large solid wheels, a flat tray, and a minimal supporting structure. The wheels become the central visual element of this functional piece, a playful reinvention of a traditional trolley. Chariot is made easily portable with a hidden handle in the curve of its support structure.

CABINET with 9 DRAWERS (MASONITE MEMORIAM)
Stockholm, Sweden
DESIGNER: **Folkform**, PRODUCER: **Svenskt Tenn**

Stockholm studio Folkform's limited-edition Masonite Memoriam cabinet is made with some of the last Masonite produced in Sweden in 2011, in combination with recovered Masonite boards from 1929. Produced exclusively for legendary Swedish manufacturer Svenskt Tenn, the cabinet is an experiment with the material, addressing issues of sustainability in design. Folkform and Svensk Tenn produced a limited edition of the cabinets in 2012.

SPIN STOOL

Stockholm, Sweden

DESIGNER:**Staffan Holm**, PRODUCER: **Swedese**

In his words, Swedish designer Staffan Holm has always been fascinated with "the poetry of crafts as well as the wonders of new technology." He says, "For me, great design has never been all about practical functions, but more about emotional ones." Throughout his interior architecture, industrial design, and furniture design practice, Holm makes spaces and products that are timeless, useful, and intelligent. For instance, Spin is a lightweight stool that can be stacked in an infinite spiral — at once creative, visually stunning, and remarkably practical.

IMEÜBLE GEOMETRIC STORAGE SYSTEM

Oslo, Norway
DESIGNER: **Bjørn Jørund Blikstad**

The Norwegian word for furniture is *møbel,* meaning "mobile" or "movable". Bjørn Jørun Blikstad's Imeüble is a modular storage device that borrows from this etymology and plays with the concept of movability — it is made to be mounted on a wall, thus becoming immobile, yet it consists of a series of interchangeable parts to be swapped in and out within this framework. Creating an illusion of skewed three-dimensional cubic space, the multicolored storage system is attention-getting and pragmatic. It was launched at the Stockholm Furniture Fair 2012 to great acclaim.

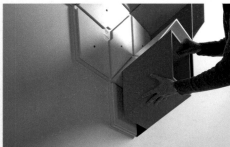

COLLECT 2011 CABINET

Huskvarna, Sweden
DESIGNER: **Sara Larsson**, PRODUCER: **A2**

Since its launch in 2009, the Swedish furniture brand A2 has pursued its vision to realize ideas that are a bit daring and different. Focusing on material selection and manufacturing its products only locally in Småland, Sweden, A2 has developed a strong identity and reputation for high quality. Designer Sarah Larsson's bright yellow Cabinet 2011 is a perfect example of the brand's approach: eye-catching yet functional. A follow-up to Larsson's white Cabinet 2010, this colorful update provides a new design option for a new year.

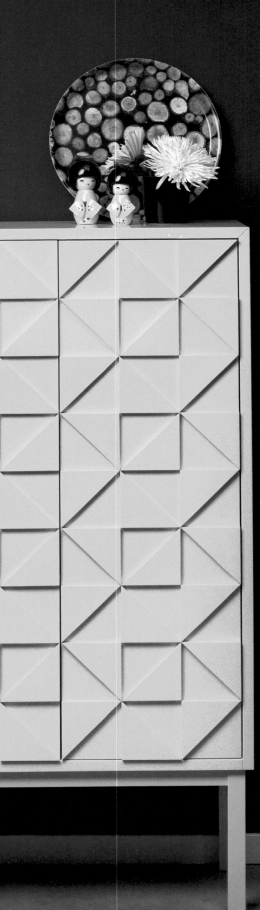

MHY
Copenhagen, Denmark
DESIGNER: **Norway Says**, PRODUCER: **Muuto**

With its playful shape and compact size, the Mhy lamp can be mounted alone, in clusters, or in rows above a table, in a hallway, or anywhere in the home. The form of Muuto's Mhy was inspired by characters from children's literature. The pendant lamp is available in several colors.

MAYOR SOFA
Copenhagen, Denmark
DESIGNER: **Arne Jacobsen**, PRODUCER: **&tradition**

&tradition is a Danish design company that produces both classic design objects by household names like Arne Jacobsen and Verner Panton and also gives voice to contemporary designers. Among the best-loved objects made by the company is the Mayor sofa, an original Arne Jacobsen design with a visible solid oak frame and upholstered cushions in either fabric or leather according to the buyer's aesthetic.

Hay was established in 2002 with the ambitious goal of returning Danish furniture design to its innovative heyday of the 1950s and 1960s. Hay strives to make good design accessible on an international level by keeping their trademark designs affordable — as well as promoting the originality of young talents alongside work by established designers. In 2011 Hay relaunched a series of Danish furniture classics originally made for the Danish Consumer's Cooperative Society (FDB). The collection includes such pieces as the flexible C44 table, with a soap-treated solid beech frame and reversible MDF tabletop, the high-backed J110 chair, and the stained solid beech J107 chair.

NORTHERN DELIGHTS

SCANDINAVIAN HOMES, INTERIORS AND DESIGN

This book was conceived, edited, and designed by Gestalten.

Edited by Emma Fexeus, Sven Ehmann, and Robert Klanten
Preface and chapter introductions by Emma Fexeus
Designer profiles by Alisa Kotmair
Project descriptions by Elvia Pyburn-Wilk

Cover by Nicole Kuderer
Cover images: Front: Villa Asserbo by Eentileen (photo: Karsten Damstedt); Back: Textile Collection by Ferm Living (photo: Ferm Living), Kråkmora Holmar by Claesson Koivisto Rune (photo: Åke E:son Lindman), The Apartment Showroom by The Apartment (photo: Alastair Halfide), Bellevue AJ2 and Raft Lowstool by &tradition (photo: &tradition)

Layout by Nicole Kuderer
Typefaces: Engel by Sofie Beier, Foundry: www.gestaltenfonts.com; Narziss by Hubert Jochum

Project management by Lucie Ulrich
Production management by Vinzenz Geppert
Proofreading by Transparent Language Solutions

Printed by Livonia Print, Riga
Made in Europe

Published by Gestalten, Berlin 2013
ISBN 978-3-89955-472-4

© Die Gestalten Verlag GmbH & Co. KG, Berlin 2013

For more information, please visit www.gestalten.com.

Bibliographic information published by the Deutsche Nationalbibliothek. The Deutsche Nationalbibliothek lists this publication in the Deutsche Nationalbibliografie; detailed bibliographic data are available online at www.dnb.d-nb.de.

None of the content in this book was published in exchange for payment by commercial parties or designers; Gestalten selected all included work based solely on its artistic merit.

This book was printed on paper certified by the FSC®.

Gestalten is a climate-neutral company. We collaborate with the non-profit carbon offset provider myclimate (www.myclimate.org) to neutralize the company's carbon footprint produced through our worldwide business activities by investing in projects that reduce CO_2 emissions (www.gestalten.com/myclimate).